DR. RILEY'S
BOX OF
TRICKS

DR. RILEY'S
BOX OF
TRICKS

80 UNCOMMON SOLUTIONS
FOR EVERYDAY PARENTING PROBLEMS

Douglas A. Riley, Ed.D.
Licensed Clinical Psychologist

Da Capo
LIFE
LONG

A Member of the Perseus Books Group

Typeset in 11.5 point Warnock Pro Light by the Perseus Books Group

Cataloging-in-Publication data for this book is available from the Library of Congress.

First Da Capo Press edition 2011
ISBN: 978-0-7382-1428-3
E-Book ISBN: 978-0-7382-1480-1

Published by Da Capo Press
A Member of the Perseus Books Group
www.dacapopress.com

Da Capo Press books are available at special discounts for bulk purchases in the U.S. by corporations, institutions, and other organizations. For more information, please contact the Special Markets Department at the Perseus Books Group, 2300 Chestnut Street, Suite 200, Philadelphia, PA 19103, or call (800) 810-4145, ext. 5000, or e-mail special.markets@perseusbooks.com.

To frustrated parents everywhere.
Thank you for inviting me into your home.

CONTENTS

CONTENTS

CONTENTS

CONTENTS

CONTENTS

INTRODUCTION

Listen to some parenting advice from one of the smartest people of the modern era: "Insanity is doing the same thing over and over again and expecting different results." That quote is attributed to Albert Einstein, by the way.

Here's what else the good Herr Doktor might have told you: "If you've given your child the same old time-out and taken away the same old toys and restricted him from the same old video games and still he continues to drive you nuts, maybe it's you who needs to change, not him."

I vividly remember the event that changed everything for me, both as a parent and a child psychologist. It occurred some fifteen years ago when my wife, two young sons, and I were on our way home from Washington, D.C., where we had spent an enjoyable but exhausting day at the Smithsonian. It wasn't long before traffic on the infamous beltway turned to stop-and-go. Inch by inch we crept for over an hour, and then I noticed that the light had come on to indicate we were low on gas. Against my better judgment I had decided not to look for gas in the city, but to wait until we got farther south on the freeway. Bad decision. Now, with no exit in sight and only miles and miles of cars stretching into the distance, traffic finally came to a complete halt. Just stopped. It was clear that we were going nowhere for a very long time. Taking a deep breath, I turned off the ignition and there we sat in silence. "I have to go to the bathroom," volunteered Sam, our youngest. "And pretty bad, too."

Born with a perfect sense of timing, our older son, Collin, eight years old at the time, decided to make what became known in our family's folklore as "The Noise." "Oooiiii-innnkkkkk . . ."

The sound was something between a bleat and a groan and a screech. Understand that Collin had a history of coming up with obnoxious noises. We had heard him make plenty of them before—but this noise! It was enough to make every cell in your body recoil. I looked in the rearview mirror and saw the pleased look on his face. "Ooooooooiiiinnkkkk," he groaned again.

"Stop it!" we all said in unison. "Please stop it right now!" Collin waited a few moments, just enough to get our hopes up, and then out it came, this time even more drawn out and exaggerated than before: "Oooooooooiiiiiiiiinnnnkkkkk . . ."

"Collin!" we all said again, turning to face him—precisely the reaction he was hoping for. His eyes were glazed with mischief and his smile was positively sly. "But I *can't* stop," he said, shrugging his shoulders. "No matter how hard I try, *it just keeps coming out. It just keeps—*"

"One more time, and you're going straight to bed when we get home," I threatened. "No computer. No snacks . . ."

"That's OK, Dad, because I actually *want* to go to bed," he said, smirking—pushing the limits even further. "Maybe then I can stop saying oiiiiinnnnnnnnkkkkkkkk."

Like any parent pushed to the breaking point by a child, my blood pressure began to rise and the desire to reach back and give him a smack was undeniable—very much not in keeping with the way a child psychologist should think during such moments.

It was obvious that ignoring this particular noise wasn't about to work, because he made it with such gusto and obvious enjoyment. We'd tried the ignoring technique many times. Along with time-out and no computer usage and no snacks and on and on and on. And we had tried yelling too, but as every parent knows, yelling is never pleasant and often takes parents to a level they regret. Nevertheless, I could feel that urge to yell coming. Then Sam began to cry from the backseat, "Mom, does this mean that Collin is *never* going to be able to stop saying that stupid word?"

And that's when the lights turned on for me. After a few moments of thought I said, "Well, Sam, I guess none of us realized the severity of the situation—you know, Collin's inability to stop saying irritating words. It must be awful for him. So look, when we get home, I'll have him stand in front of his mirror and say that word for fifteen minutes straight, without a break. We obviously need to help him drain all those oinks out of his system, and that's the only way to do it."

Collin looked at me rather coyly and smiled. "That'll be fun!" he said. "I like making that noise."

"Fifteen minutes!" I said back.

"Oiiiiiiiinnnnnnnnnkkkkkk," he bleated in response. "Oii-iiiiinnnnnnnnnnkkkkkkk oooooiiiinnnnnkkkkkkk oooiiiinn-nnkkkkkk . . ."

"Poor little guy can't stop," I said to my wife. "He really needs our help."

By the time we got home that night (yes, we did find a gas station in the nick of time), Collin and Sam were blessedly asleep in the backseat. I resisted the temptation to put Collin to bed, and instead took him to the full-length mirror that hung over his door. I instructed him to stand in front of the mirror. "OK, let's begin the draining process," I said. "I believe you know what to do."

Collin grinned sheepishly, took a deep breath, and began. "Oooiiinnkkkk," he bleated.

"Again, please."

"Ooooooiiiiiiiiinnnnnnnnkkkkkkk."

I nodded for him to continue, knowing clearly that I was on to something. He made The Noise with gusto for the first three minutes or so. But after that he began to peter out, say-ing he was getting tired, that the sound was hurting his throat, that he had learned his lesson, and so on. I assured him the draining process was necessary, and it was my experience that it would not be complete until the last second of the fifteen minutes was over. Only then would his system be fully drained of the oinks.

The last time Collin Riley uttered "Ooooooiiiiinnnnnnnn-kkkkk," standing there in front of the mirror, was the last time we ever heard that particular sound again. Period. Nada. Over and done. Or so I thought.

The next weekend he decided to give it another go, mainly out of that irresistible desire to bug his brother. I found myself at a crossroads, thinking my draining intervention had failed. Then I had another epiphany about draining: I apologized to him profusely. "I am so sorry," I said. "I thought I'd be able to drain all of that noise out of your system last week by having you do it for fifteen minutes, but it looks like I failed. There are definitely still plenty of oinks left in you. This time we'll just have to try harder. Today I'll let you stand in front of your mirror and make The Noise for thirty minutes. If thirty minutes doesn't drain it all out of your system, I'll be forced to admit I failed again, so then we will have to go to forty-five minutes. And then after that to sixty minutes, and so on."

I truly can say now that we have never heard The Noise again, and for years afterward, if either of my sons did something repetitive to bug the other (making other noises, making faces, saying words or phrases repeatedly, making gestures, etc.), all I'd have to say was "Would you like me to help you drain that out of your system?"

"No, Dad," they would say emphatically. "We'll stop."

So now I'm on a rescue mission. My target? Moms and dads who are so worn down by the everyday battles of parenting that all of life's joy has left the building, so to speak. And you know the battles I'm talking about. It's not just obnoxious noises. It's heated arguments with little attorneys one-fourth your age or one-half your size over why bedtime should be midnight instead of nine; it's plates of chips and cheese under the sofa spawning mold colonies that resemble alien life forms; it's your six-year-old screaming that her brother is looking at her or that he's breathing too loud; it's your teenage son's inability to lift the toilet seat. It's when your home gets turned into a war zone over which child controls the TV channel changer or the video game controller, when in actuality both of them ought to be hitting the books because their grades stink. But when you ask them what they learned at school, the only answer you get is "I don't know" or "Stuff." If this quagmire sounds familiar, like most parents you need some methods that actually work. What you need is a Box of Tricks.

This book is for busy parents who don't have the time or the emotional energy to think up new strategies to grab the attention of basically good children whose behavior has gotten out of hand. (However, if you discover along the way that you are talented in coming up with new methods of your own to get your child's attention, I'd like to hear about them so they can be included in future editions of this book. More about that in the last chapter.) Getting their attention is, after all, the biggest trick a parent needs to master. Until that is accomplished, there will be no change.

Ultimately, it goes like this: you can lecture Junior repeatedly about how kitty doesn't like it when he bothers her. However, he is not likely to really learn his lesson in any sort of deep, meaningful way until kitty does something dramatic. As Mark Twain is claimed to have said, "A man who carries a cat by the tail learns something he can learn in no other way."

My methods provide children with a gentler version of this real-world lesson, using humorous talk combined with painless but unforgettable consequences. You'll learn about the boy who was "grounded from his mouth" because of his excessive arguing. You'll learn about the girl whose room was used as the family laundry hamper until she finally agreed to stop throwing her clothes all over the floor. You'll learn that it's OK to charge kids for asking them more than twice to pick up their coat or book bag and put it away. You'll learn surprisingly effective ways to deal with kids who yell at you, kids who lie, kids who wreck trips with their backseat combat, and more.

So, what should you expect if you decide to go ahead and open the Box of Tricks? Expect your kids, at first, to be wide-eyed and shocked that you would even think about using such methods on them. Then, as you discuss the tricks, you'll find that most children have trouble hiding their smiles or their laughter. That's because everything in this book is unconventional, always contains a good dose of humor or irony, and is thoroughly unexpected.

Be ready to encounter your own smiles and laughter too, because the tricks will remind you clearly that most of the things you're fighting about with your child are behaviors that can be described as "painfully normal." Sure, it bugs the dickens out of you to struggle with your child about not remembering to make up his bed before he leaves for school, or feed his pets, or turn in his homework. But what parent doesn't go through these arguments? My tricks not only help parents find rapid solutions to these problems, they get parents into the frame of mind that everything will turn out just fine in the long run.

And last but not least . . . once your child discovers that you still have a sense of humor buried in there under all the layers of frustration and fighting and high-volume arguing that comes with parenting, his or her viewpoint of you changes. Your child will experience you as much more approachable and a lot more enjoyable to interact with. And, in its own odd way, your willingness to use the tricks in this book will help you arrive at that point you had hoped to arrive at to begin with, the point where you can talk and they will listen.

A WHOLE
NEW STRATEGY

"Change in all things is sweet."
—*Aristotle*

The Five Rules of
Parent Reprogramming

If you want to learn to use the types of techniques that worked so well with my son and that appear in this book, you may need some reprogramming. There are five simple rules you must accept:

1. Stay calm. Rid your mind of the thought that turning up the volume will enhance communication with your child. At some point little children become frightened of you, and older ones simply turn up the volume on their iPods, reducing you to background noise.

2. Stop arguing! Arguing with kids deludes them into believing they are your equal. The more you argue, the more they will too. Stand in front of a mirror and practice saying this: "Sorry. It's not my job to argue with people your age."

3. Don't continue to try to reason with a child who is obviously not listening. Get over the fact that you can't rely on the same type of reason and logic that makes you so successful in all the other areas of your life when dealing with him. You can employ a line of logic powerful enough to raise the dead or suspend gravity, and still he will look at you like you're the village idiot.

4. Make it fun. Get back to the business of having some serious fun with your child. Having fun together always leads to fewer problems and better relationships. And last but not least . . .

5. Keep it light. If you don't have a sense of humor about all the things your kids have done and will continue to do to drive you nuts, go rent one, buy one, or get yourself into humor restoration therapy.

A Basic Primer in Using Tricks

As you read through the various tricks, you'll get the hang of how to use them in your home. In many cases, all you'll have to do is simply describe the trick you're thinking about using to your child. You'll be surprised at how often he or she will promise to change rather than have you go through with it. In other cases you might decide to just read the trick right from the book to your child and then talk about it. If you actually have to go ahead and use the trick, chances are you won't have to use it more than once or twice before your child promises to change. And sometimes there are those situations in which no advance warning is necessary. Just go ahead and put the trick into operation.

Be careful not to overwhelm your child by using too many tricks at a time. Choose your battles wisely, and use no more than one trick a day. By keeping your other tricks in reserve, you give your child the impression that you have an endless supply.

Any trick you use will contain three steps. First, you'll have to get your child's attention by making him or her aware of the possible consequence that can happen unless a particular behavior is changed. (It is the fact that the consequence is so new and unexpected that will rivet your child's attention to what you are saying.) Second, you'll need to let your child know in the friendliest possible way that you are not bluffing. Third, you will always, always, always offer a "soft landing." This is when you give your child an out, an option of voluntarily changing his or her behavior in order to completely avoid the consequences you're warning him or her about.

Let me give you an example: Kevin was a nine-year-old boy who was driving his mother batty with his arguing. After

I got to know him, I looked at him one day and said, "Since we're not making too much headway with all this arguing you're doing with your mother, I suppose we'll have to try grounding you from your mouth." I wish you could have seen the look of disbelief on his face.

I explained in detail that his mother was to use this intervention for one hour at a time, once per day, until his excessive arguing ceased. For the entire hour he would not be allowed to talk, drink, or eat. Any meals or snacks planned for that time would have to be delayed. If he had to communicate with his mom about anything, he would have to write it down on a piece of paper. If he broke the silence before his time was up, he'd have to start all over.

Then I said, "You need to look at your mom and ask if she really would use a technique like Grounded from Your Mouth." He looked at her and sheepishly asked, and she nodded emphatically that she would. Then she started to laugh and smile herself, because the technique also struck her as unexpected and funny.

After that, I offered him the soft landing we talked about above. I told him if he began to change his arguing, his mother would not have to use silly methods like Grounded from Your Mouth.

The meeting ended well. I congratulated Kevin for working hard during our talk and told him how proud I was that he paid attention so well, maintained his eye contact, and never attempted to escape off into arguing or silence or answering "I don't know" whenever I asked him a question.

Kevin and his mother left the office on better footing with each other, and she told me later that just the thought that his mother would use such unusual techniques seemed to keep his arguing in check.

An Advanced Primer in Using Tricks

You'll notice that the tricks employ different types of logic, depending on the situation. Let's look at these quickly.

Draining. We'll use this when kids are doing things that they know for sure are bothering others. One boy bugged everyone in his class by insisting he had the "right" to hum quite loudly while working at his desk. He adamantly refused to stop, even though everyone seated close to him had begged him to knock it off. I told him that in order to help him correct this bad habit, we would need to have him hum for fifteen minutes straight in his bedroom to drain all the humming out. When this didn't work, his parents moved him to thirty minutes, with the promise that forty-five was just around the corner if he kept bothering the other children.

Apology and Repetition. Zero in on a behavior that needs to be changed but is not necessarily being done to purposefully bother others. If you have a child who slams the door, go to her with an apology. Tell her it was your job to teach her how to close doors, and you've obviously failed. Now you intend to help her learn to do it correctly, and the only way to learn

is through lots of repetitions—in this case, opening and closing the door repeatedly until she gets it right.

Techniques based on apology and repetition are particularly useful when children claim they're "not able to help
it." Rather than yell at your child that he can control himself
but just doesn't want to, explain that all the repetitions will
finally help him gain control. It will be a whole lot easier on
your nerves and will drive the point home to him in a way
he can't ignore.

A Taste of Your Own Medicine. This is a concept you're no
doubt familiar with from your own childhood. Some kids are
simply so unable to see the impact of their behavior on others that all the talk in the world gets parents exactly nowhere.
We'll use tricks like making your pokey kid wait, or bugging
the kid who loves to bug everyone else.

What You Can Expect

In particular, after you begin to mention these tricks, expect
some pushback. Your children aren't going to easily believe
you've abandoned traditional parenting tools like time-out
and grounding in favor of more exotic techniques. Expect
them to say or do things in an attempt to make you believe
your tricks won't work on them, or that they won't go along
with anything you come up with. All of this is fine, and nothing to get upset about. Most children have to test how far
they can push the limits.

If your child refuses to go along with a trick, your next step is to move on to the types of tricks that don't require his or her direct participation. Say, for example, your daughter will not go along with practicing how to close her bedroom door properly. Rather than blowing your top, you can always explain that because of all the damage she's doing to her doorjamb, you will simply have to remove the door from its hinges. At some point in the process, your child will tell you she's finally gotten the point. As usual, if her promises seem genuine, give her a soft landing.

When Not to Use Tricks

I want you to mentally repeat after me: any trick I use will be physically and psychologically harmless to my children, regardless of how angry I happen to be. In fact, tricks are never to be used when you're angry. They must be reserved for when you're clear-headed and still in touch with that sense of humor I talked about earlier. If your child has managed to push all your buttons and you are about to explode, take a deep breath, walk into the other room, down a glass of cold water, take a quick walk, watch some mindless television, etc. Only after you are calm should you even think about implementing a trick.

There are also other points I'm quite serious about, things you must pay attention to:

- Don't use tricks on mean, snarly, juvenile-delinquent-type kids. I am speaking specifically about the type of child who likes to hurt and bully others, or the angry type of child who clearly has no respect for the adult world and is ready, willing, and able to demonstrate it at the drop of a hat. They will experience the tricks in this book as personal attacks. Instead, these children should be in counseling with a well-seasoned therapist who specializes in children with behavior disorders.

• Do not use tricks on any child who is developmentally challenged or on the autistic spectrum or not intellectually capable of analyzing the impact of his or her behavior on others. These children will not be able to get the point you are trying to make with them. Instead, they will be confused by your behavior. If they need to change particular behaviors, turn instead to a therapist with expertise in developmental disabilities and behavior modification.

• Do not use tricks on children who are clearly depressed, especially those who have thoughts of harming themselves or those who have been diagnosed with bipolar disorder. Depressed children almost always suffer from a negative self-image and are locked in a struggle to feel good about themselves. They experience the world as a hostile place. First and foremost, they need your kindness, understanding, and patience. They may also benefit from cognitive behavior therapy, or a consult with a good child psychiatrist.

• Do not use the Box of Tricks on highly anxious children, especially children who display obsessive compulsive symptoms or who are extremely explosive. Highly anxious children are always worried about the bad things they're convinced are going to happen sooner or later. Because all of their emotional energies are tied up in trying to solve problems from the future, they may fail to see the humor in what you're trying to do in the present. It will be much better to talk to them gently about their worries and their fears. You may be surprised at how this will lead to better behavior from them in general. As with their depressed counterparts, it will be best to seek professional help.

I repeat: the techniques in this book are meant to be used on healthy, normal, happy kids, age six to fourteen, who have a sense of humor and the ability to be enjoyable, but who have hit a hardheaded stage and are driving you nuts. So, if your child is the type who is ripping it up at home but the neighbors and teachers generally tell you what a joy he or she is, keep reading.

And now, time to open The Box . . .

WHEN YOUR
KIDS IGNORE YOU

"Children aren't happy with nothing to ignore,
and that's what parents were created for."

—*Ogden Nash, American poet*

One of the things that irritate parents the most is when their children ignore them. It can feel downright insulting and sometimes even heartbreaking, particularly given the time and energy most parents pour into their children. It fact, it's easy to take the insult personally, to think that your child might not love or respect or appreciate you, or to think that he or she might actually be ignoring you on purpose just to bug the heck out of you (which, of course, is entirely possible and likely). But don't let yourself get too upset about being ignored. A certain amount of testing the limits just comes with being a kid. You did it, I did it, and look how well we turned out!

Trick: Two Times for Free

Use It On: Children age six to twelve who are doing their best to pretend you don't exist.

When to Employ: When you're beyond tired of asking children ten times to pick up coats, put away shoes, or properly store action figures or miniature cars or Barbies or anything else with edges and corners that you manage to step on when the lights are out and you're barefooted. You know the drill.

What You'll Need: Some righteous indignation; a sense of humor; some quarters; and a lengthy list of jobs that need to get done around your house.

Your assignment is to bring your child back to reality by teaching him or her that while you are loving and tolerant, you are not to be ignored. This chapter is short, but potent. The trick you're about to learn is sure to bring a halt to your child's belief that listening to you is optional.

OK, let's start with a rapid solution for being ignored. As long as we're at it, let's introduce my poster boy for making parents repeat themselves—Gregory—because he's a good example of a boy who had to be asked, told, and threatened repeatedly to do anything his mom needed him to do. Gregory was seven, and this is what his typical interaction with his mother was like:

Mom: "How many times do I have to tell you? Pick up your coat? Pick! Up! Your! Coat! Which one of those words don't you understand? You're driving me nuts!"

Gregory: "Mom, quit bugging me! I already told you I'll do it! Just give me a minute! Jeez!"

Five agonizing minutes later . . .

Mom: "Gregory! If you don't pick up that coat I'm going to . . . I'm going to . . . I don't know *what* I'm going to do with you."

If you have a child like Gregory and feel tempted to yell and scream at him the next time he makes you repeat yourself, try this instead: look at him calmly and say, "I have decided to use a program with you called 'Two Times for Free.' Here is how it works: from now on, I will be willing to ask you two times to do what I need you to do. However, if I have to ask you more than twice, I will charge you. Now, please pick up your coat and hang it in the closet. Thank you very much!"

Once you do this, be prepared for your child to look at you strangely, like a third eye has opened on your forehead. Give him two minutes to reorient and to comply. Say nothing more. If he does as asked, great! But if two minutes go by and he has regrouped his defenses sufficiently to give you his usual response, which is to ignore you completely, then you'll have to make your second request.

This in itself brings up an exceptionally important issue: what makes you think if you ask the second time just like you asked the first that the outcome will be any different?

Your second request *must* take a much different form than your first:

You (still remaining calm): "Please come here and give me eyeballs." (That's my way of saying "look at me and pay attention.")

Child: "Aw, Mom . . ."

You: "I am now asking you for the second time to pick up your coat and hang it up. Do you understand what I want you to do?"

Child: "Yes."

You (just to make sure your child is listening): "What is it I want you to do?"

Child: "You want me to pick up my coat and hang it up."

You: "Yes. Please make a smart decision."

If two more minutes go by and your child is still managing to ignore you, or is arguing, the game is on. This is what you say next: "I've already asked you twice to pick up your coat and hang it up. In a moment, I'll ask you to do it again. However, because I've already asked you two times for free, I'm now going to charge you twenty-five cents for asking you again. (For the older kids, fifty cents to a dollar may be more appropriate.) Please go up to your room and get me a quarter."

Your child will likely say something along this line: "But, Mom, I'll pick it up now. This quarter thing is *stooopid*!"

You: "As I just said, I've already asked you two times for free to hang up your coat. Please go get that quarter, put it in my hand, and then I'll ask you for the third time."

Expect your child to go stomping up the steps (more about how to cure this later), return angrily with a quarter, and slam it into your hand. You then say, "Thank you very much! Now, please pick your coat up and hang it in the closet. And let me remind you, if I have to ask you again, I will charge you another quarter."

There are variations of Two Times for Free. Let's suppose, for instance, that your child does not have a stash of money in her room, or that you want to make your point in a somewhat more dramatic fashion. You can tell your child that you have all the quarters you need and have instead decided to charge her twenty-five cents' worth of *work* for asking a third time. Explain that twenty-five-cent jobs might involve scrubbing a toilet, or wiping off the kitchen table and countertops, or vacuuming one room, or cleaning one window, or emptying the dishwasher, or cleaning out the cat box, or sweeping the kitchen floor. Tell her she will have to pay you immediately for asking a third time by doing one of these jobs. (Also tell her you might even let her choose which job she gets to do from among the list.) Remind her that after she does the job she will still have to do what you originally asked her to do—hang up her coat.

If you decide to use Two Times for Free, you might find that your son or daughter will try to mount a defense, just like Gregory did. His argument was that the quarter system was illegal and was a form of slave labor. He shouted at his mother, "Why should I pay to do my chores? That doesn't make any sense! You're just going to make me more angry!"

I can only imagine his satisfaction with himself at that moment, no doubt believing that he had absolutely destroyed his mother's position with his slick reasoning.

His mom told me she had anticipated he would take things in that direction, and answered him straightforwardly by saying if he did what she asked in a timely manner, he would never have to pay a penny. In this regard, it was actually his choice.

Did Gregory ever become Mr. Compliant? No. Did this trick cure his arguing forever? Probably not. But it sure put a dent in his mother's having to repeat her requests. It brought the point home that things had to change in a new, sane way—one that got his attention and preserved his mother's vocal cords.

YELLERS, SCREAMERS, INSULTERS, CURSERS, AND THOSE EVER-LOVING LITTLE MUMBLERS

"Laughter and tears are both responses to frustration and exhaustion.
I myself prefer to laugh, since there is less cleaning up to do afterward."

—*Kurt Vonnegut, American writer and humorist*

Do you have a communication problem in your home? Do you have a child who has decided to try yelling at you to see if he or she can get away with it? Do you have a child who is testing the limits by letting slip the occasional bad word? Or, at the other end of the spectrum, do you have a child who puts so little effort into his communication that you can hardly understand him? You are far from alone. Hundreds of parents have told me what a struggle it is to keep their children polite and communicative. In this chapter, we'll discuss some *new* options.

Trick: Pump Up the Volume

Use It On: Children between six and fourteen who've come to believe you're hard of hearing.

When to Employ: After you have repeatedly told your child to stop yelling at you, because you can hear just fine (which obviously your child didn't hear, so maybe *he or she* is the one whose ears don't work too well), and now you want to try something radical.

What You'll Need: It is strongly advised that you pick up a set of earplugs at your local drugstore. They're cheap.

If you have a child who believes it's OK to yell at you, then you need to hear about Dan. He was a burly fourteen-year-old who was completely obsessed with TV wrestling. In fact, he loved to act out his wrestler *look* for me, the one he claimed he used at school to intimidate the other boys: he would lower his head, lock eyes with me, and begin to shake and vibrate, as if under the influence of some torrential flood of testosterone. I sort of expected him to lunge at any moment, which was exactly the point. He wanted the other boys to think that his ability to control himself was worn as thin as an atom, and that there was almost nothing preventing him from pounding them into the size and shape of a pancake if they crossed him even a little bit.

Here's the problem: Dan had decided his muscles and size made him his mother's equal, and so he had taken to yelling at her constantly. Everything he said to her was punctuated with a snarl.

I had her tell him that since he obviously believed that shouting was the only way he could communicate with her, he would now have to shout *everything* he wanted her to hear. "Wiped it out almost immediately," she told me later.

I have laughed for years over what dinner must have been like at their house:

Dan: "Pass the salt, please."

Mom: No response.

Dan: "Mom, I said pass the salt, please."

Mom: No response.

Dan: **"PASS THE SALT, PLEASE!"**

Mom: *Still* no response.

Dan: **"PAAAASSS THE SAALLLTT, PLEEEZE!"**

Mom: "Oh, OK, here you go."

Over the years I have told hundreds of screaming children Dan's story. Almost every one of them ends up shaking their head and smiling, saying they hope their parents won't use anything like Pump Up the Volume on them.

Trick: Don't Stand, Don't Stand, Don't Stand So Close to Me . . .

Use It On: More of those six- to fourteen-year-olds who have taken to yelling at you but who are still loveable at heart.

When to Employ: When you're really tired of yelling back, because yelling doesn't work and it makes you feel bad about yourself to boot.

What You'll Need: That sense of humor that we continue to mention, and some cough drops.

The next time your child or teen starts to yell at you, go stand very, very close to her. Do your best not to laugh. When she asks what you are doing, tell her since she obviously believes you don't hear very well, you'll stand really close so she doesn't have to shout and end up with a sore throat. Offer her a cough drop and tell her you love her dearly, but you intend to do this every time she pumps up the volume. Tell her she should be grateful to you for being so concerned about those precious vocal cords of hers.

Trick: My Ears Don't Work Too Well

Use It On: Your basically good kid, age six to ten, who is going through that phase of thinking he can yell mean things at you.

When to Employ: When you're sick and tired of being told off by your little darling after a long day of cooking, cleaning, working at the office, taking kids to soccer practice, helping with homework, etc., etc.

What You'll Need: The ability to not overreact when your child says something truly mean. You'll also need more earplugs, a list of chores you need done, a straight face, and a willingness to follow through, even if it ends up hurting a little.

The first thing you've got to learn to do with kids who develop the tendency to shout mean things at you is to not take it personally. If you can do that, then you can successfully do the second thing, which is to matter-of-factly mention to your child during a calm period that your ears don't seem to be working all that well anymore. Say you don't understand why, and just leave it at that. Then, the next time your child decides to scream something mean at you, simply "misunderstand" what he or she said.

There are two versions of this trick, a "silly" version that works particularly well with young screamers, and a more edgy version you can use with kids eight and up. The silly version goes like this:

Child: "I hate you!"

You: "I'm sorry, you know my ears just don't work as well as they used to. It sounded like you just said you have a cucumber in your nose! That's the strangest thing I've ever heard."

Child: "No! I said I hate you!"

You: "What? You just said it again. I can't believe you think you have a cucumber in your nostril! That's just weird!"

What usually happens when parents use the silly version of My Ears Don't Work Too Well is that sooner or later everyone starts laughing. This decreases the tension, and over the long run decreases the hurling of insults in your direction because your child can no longer delude herself into thinking she has achieved some sort of victory over you via volume and nastiness.

Then there is the edgy version. In this version, when your child starts yelling or screaming at you, you stick to what you *thought* you heard with those faulty ears of yours. For example:

Child: "You're the worst mother on the planet! I wish I lived at Suzie's!"

You: "My goodness. It sounded like you just said you wanted to vacuum the living room."

Child: "You know that's not what I said! You heard me! This is just another one of your dumb tricks!"

You: "I am certain that's what you said, and you said it quite loudly too. In fact, you screamed it, so there's not much chance I'd misunderstand. I think vacuuming the floor is a *wonderful* offer on your part. Thank you so much!"

Child: "No, that is *not* what I said!"

You: "Well, that is what I heard you say, and I have to agree that the floor *does* need vacuuming. So please go get it done immediately."

Now let's play this out just a bit further. Suppose you do this with your child, and she says she will absolutely not vacuum the floor. This is where you give her a choice. Tell her she can either vacuum the floor and get it over with quickly, or she can begin to lose freedoms and privileges for the rest of the day. If she's like most kids, she will break out the vacuum. If she is muttering under her breath the whole time she's vacuuming, fine. *The main point is that she learns that it is no longer safe to yell such things at you.*

Here's another variation to use if your child calls you "dumb" or "stupid." It goes like this:

Child: "You're so dumb!"

You: "Did I just hear you say that I'm too dumb to figure out how to order the pizza and wings I had planned for dinner tonight? Oh well, guess leftovers will have to do."

Be sure to follow through with the leftovers, no matter how badly you had your heart set on pizza and wings.

Trick: Shutting Up

Use It On: Children age eight to fourteen who tell you to "shut up" or "be quiet," or use some similarly rude statement on you.

When to Employ: Soon after you get over the shock of being talked to like this by your child.

What You'll Need: Some index cards and a pen or pencil.

Do you have a child who tells you to shut up on a routine basis? No parent should accept this type of behavior from a child, because it means something is seriously out of balance in the family. But if you do have a basically good kid who is making this mistake with you and you have exhausted reason, logic, and talk in an attempt to get things to change, here's a trick to use: tell your child that the next time she says this, you intend to fall silent for the next hour, regardless of what else she says to you. Tell her you will say nothing to her unless, as one mom told me, she is bleeding or her hair is on fire. (You will, of course, be perfectly able to talk to any other child in the home who is treating you as you deserve to be treated.)

Tell her that when she tries to get you to talk, your only response will be to hold up an index card on which you have written, "I have shut up. During my silence you may not go anywhere, consume any food or drink, or use any device that requires electricity." Tell her that without a doubt, you will stick to your guns. It goes something like this:

Mom: "I'm tired of you telling me to shut up. So guess what? The next time you tell me to shut up, I will."

Child (smirking): "OK. Shut up, Mom."

Mom: Holds up the card.

Child: "Mom, this is really dumb."

Mom: Card stays up.

Child: "Knock it off, Mom."

Mom: Makes the motion of zipping her lips and points to the words "I have shut up."

Suppose you go through with this, and sometime in the near future your child again tells you to shut up. Use your card again, but this time for two hours. Shutting up, odd as it might sound, will eventually be painful enough to your child that it should prompt a real discussion about just how inappropriate it is for her to talk to you this way.

Trick: Misunnerstaninmblrs
(Translation: Misunderstanding Mumblers)

Use It On: Kids six to fourteen who mumble; kids who talk with their fingers in their mouths; kids who talk so low you can't hear what they're saying.

When to Employ: After your child has repeated himself for the fourth time and you still have no idea what the subject matter is.

What You'll Need: Your child will supply the fingers and the mumbling.

Here's a twist you can use on misunderstanding: lots of boys go through a stage in which they almost seem to make themselves hard to understand on purpose. They talk with their hands or arms in front of their mouths, or put their fingers in their mouths at the same time they're speaking, or speak so low you can hardly hear them. If you have a child who mumbles too much and does not have an actual speech impediment that makes his communications difficult to understand, stop trying so hard to translate. Rather, make sure you misunderstand him *completely*, throwing in a bit of humor. Pretty soon he'll clear up his communications. For example:

Child: "Iwangotooovieswidtmafriend."

You: "You just said your best friend's name is Hoover? That's a very interesting name."

Child: "SnotwhatIsaidIsaidIwanttogotothemovieswith-myfriends."

You: "What? You said you want to buy a *ploover*? What is a ploover?"

Child: "*No*, Mom. What . . . I . . . said . . . was . . . I . . . want . . . to . . . go . . . to . . . the . . . movies . . . with . . . my . . . friends."

You: "Oh, now I get it. When you mumble I can't understand a word you say. Of course you can go. Have fun."

Do this just a few times, and you will teach your mumbler that mumbling around you is more trouble than it's worth.

Trick: The Frickin' Trick

Use It On: Young wanna-be cursers, ten to fourteen.

When to Employ: When your tweener or teen is trying out semi-curse words at a frequency that has gone too far.

What You'll Need: The ability to tolerate repetition.

Let me tell you about ten-year-old Nate. He was at that point in his development when boys are just dying to try out cursing, but they're also trying to keep it clean enough to stay out of trouble. He had taken to using the word "frickin'" frequently, particularly around his mother. She found it offensive and told him he was not allowed to use any derivative of the f-bomb around her at any time. He persisted, even using it in my office.

I don't want you to think of Nate as a bad kid. He was good-natured and funny. I told him I had a trick we could use to help him stop saying that word. His initial response was "Oh no! Not another one of your tricks!"

I told him we could do a draining procedure if we had to, the type I described in Chapter 1. I said we could give him a two-minute taste of draining the word out of his system right there in my office, just so he could see what it would be like. Then I took out my stopwatch. He was not the type of kid to throw up a lot of objections, so when I started the watch, he started draining: "Frickin'frickin'frickin'frickin'-frickin'frickin'frickin'frickin'frickin'frickin'frickin'frickin'frickin'frickin'frickin'frickin'."

While he was doing this, I was looking away so as not to give him any reinforcement and his mom was looking away so she wouldn't laugh, which she knew would egg him on. After about sixty seconds, you could tell he was beginning to tire. His cadence was changing, but he was still working away. "Frickin' frickin' frickin' frickin' frickin' frickin'."

Finally the watch hit two minutes. To be honest with you, had he been enjoying the whole thing too much, as some kids do, I would have let the watch go on to three minutes but would have told him it was two, and made a comment about just how long two minutes can feel. He said, all on his own, "I didn't think that would ever be over with."

I said, "You just had two minutes. Think about what it would feel like if your mom had you do this for fifteen minutes. Or thirty minutes. Moms can do that, you know."

I suppose we could refer to the two-minute technique as "draining lite." It works quite well for a couple of reasons. First, it demonstrates to your child that you are not kidding, that you will definitely follow through. Second, it shows what it really would be like to have to go through with a full fifteen-minute treatment of the trick. Almost always, this will make the child decide to stop doing the behavior in question. In Nate's case, the word lost its magical appeal quickly. If it looked like he was about to recapitulate, his mother would remind him that she knew the proper trick to help him stop.

Trick: #*%*! (Translation: The Potty Mouth Log)

Use It On: Any child ten and up who has decided it's safe to let some bad words slip out around you.

When to Employ: It's best to get started with this trick as soon as possible.

What You'll Need: A notebook and a writing instrument.

A mother I knew had two sons, twelve and fourteen, who would occasionally blurt out curse words around her. They would argue that it was no big deal, and say that all of their friends used the same sort of words around their parents. Or they would say that it was just a word, just a *sound*, so what's the big deal? As with most of the parents I talk about in this book, their mother had tried all of the conventional talk and punishments and inducements to get them to clean up their act, all to no avail.

This is what we did: I had her get a notebook that was kept on the kitchen counter and was opened up to a page that was headed "Foul Language that the Boys Have Used Around Their Mother." It was the official log for all the offensive words her sons said. Each time she busted one of them for bad language, he would have to write down the word and the date he said it, and sign his name by it. At first, each boy acted as if logging his cursing was no big deal, just a minor irritant and actually sort of funny. But after a few weeks, both sons got tired of having to do it and were pretty embarrassed by the evidence of how they were acting around their mother, who, for the most part, they loved dearly. Plus, they were quite afraid that someone outside the family might come in and see the notebook lying there.

In this particular instance, the mother reported that her sons ultimately stopped using bad language when she was around. It is exceptionally important, however, that you understand the difference between a child's using curse words *around* you, as opposed to using curse words *on* you. The first is pretty typical boy behavior and will respond well to tricks. The second is an indication of deeper issues between you and your child. In such instances, professional help is called for. No parent should be cursed *at* by a child.

DOOR SLAMMERS
AND
STAIR STOMPERS

All of us want our children to learn to handle their anger in appropriate ways. Displacing anger onto your house is not an option. I've met so many children who slam doors or go stomping up steps when angered that I've had to come up with techniques to bring these behaviors to a halt. Granted, it is quite normal for children to go through stages of acting this way. However, many of them fail to make the transition to learning to use their words to express their emotions. The tricks that follow will help them make this transition. However, I need to point out that if your child has already made another sort of transition—going from slamming doors or stomping up stairs to actually punching holes in walls or breaking things—tricks are not appropriate. You would be best advised to seek help from a therapist trained in anger management.

Trick: Door-Slamming Practice

Use It On: Heavy-handed children six to twelve who seem to have forgotten how to close a door properly.

When to Employ: Once it's clear that your child believes doors are the appropriate tool for demonstrating his or her displeasure with your rules, regulations, limits, and demands.

What You'll Need: Any working door will do (except a sliding one).

What can you do if you have a child whose way of showing her anger is to slam your doors, and no amount of reason and logic and talk has gotten her to stop? I hinted at this earlier and now want to get into it in more detail. First, sit her down and explain, using your knowledge of the repetition concept, that as her parent it is your job to teach her how to close doors properly, and you have obviously failed. Apologize to her profusely, all the while watching the look on her face that says she's not comfortable because you've never acted this strangely before.

Next, tell her one way you can teach her to open and close a door successfully is to have her do it twenty-five times in a row while you watch and provide friendly, constructive feedback. Explain that twenty-five times seems like a sufficient number of repetitions to help her get it right and that, after all, opening and closing a door is just one more acquired skill, like learning how to kick a soccer ball properly, or how to serve a tennis ball. Point out that even her own coaches have her do repetitions and drills because everyone knows that's how new skills are mastered.

Then reiterate that if she slams the door again after you have taken the time to teach her and provide friendly, constructive feedback, you will be forced again to admit your failure. Obviously, having her do it twenty-five times was not enough. So the next time will be fifty. Then after that, seventy-five, ultimately topping off at a limit of one hundred. Remind her that *she always has the option to simply stop slamming the door to begin with, in which case none of this will be necessary.* The final warning goes like this: "One more slam and I will go through with my plan, starting at twenty-five."

Let's play this out. Assume your child refuses to go through with the door-closing practice. This is when you give her another choice: either she goes through with the practice or you will be forced to protect her bedroom door from her because it's the one she slams the most. And the only way to do that is to take it off its hinges and store it somewhere until she learns to treat it properly.

As one slammer complained at my office, "I've lost my door!"

"No, you haven't," her dad said back. "You know exactly where it is. It's in the garage for safekeeping."

Trick: Stair-Stomper Training

Use It On: Heavy-footed kids, age six to twelve.

When to Employ: Better to do this one before they crack your stair treads, rather than after.

What You'll Need: You'll need a two-story house, condo, or apartment. If you don't live in one already, chances are slim you'll need this trick.

You can use techniques with stair stompers that are similar to the one for door slammers. What you'll need to do is pull your child aside and tell him that as his parent, it is your job to teach him how to go up and down stairs properly. Tell him you have obviously failed, and apologize repeatedly for this oversight. Then explain that you are considering having him go up and down the stairs for five minutes while you observe his particular pattern of stair-stepping in order to give him constructive feedback. Tell him the point of this is to help him prevent the kind of stomping that is *certain* to break the treads, thus costing him lots and lots of allowance money or saved-up birthday money.

Also point out that if he goes through a five-minute period of stair training but still goes stomping up the stairs the next time he's mad, you will come to him with another apology. This time you will be happy to give him ten minutes to practice. If there is another incident after that, he will deserve yet another apology, and so on. Remind him that, at your option, you can also decide to ground him from the stairs for an hour at a time, meaning it will be impossible for him to get to his room. Say that you have great faith in his ability to sooner or later get it right, and remind him that the outcome is totally in his hands.

TALES OF
MESSY ROOMS

"It is not giving children more that spoils them;
it is giving them more to avoid confrontation."

—*John Gray, American writer*

Here's another high-frequency issue at my office—kids who leave everything messy. Sometimes it's due to laziness, sometimes to obstinacy, sometimes to absentmindedness. Whatever the cause, we do not want our children to be slobs. At the same time, parents need to remain sane about what they expect from their children in the way of neatness. Don't be one of those parents who isn't satisfied until the child's room can pass the white-glove test. Many parents are surprised to learn that simply complimenting a child on her cleaning effort, even when far less than perfect, will result in the child's trying even harder to keep things neat. Likewise, I've seen many children turn into better housekeepers simply because their parents made the effort to insert a bit more fun and happiness into the household. You might be surprised at how willing a child is to pitch in with cleaning when it's done with good music blaring on the stereo instead of complaints and negativity blaring out of Mom or Dad's mouth. But if the friendly way doesn't work at your house, keep reading.

Trick: The Family Laundry Hamper

Use It On: Children eight to fourteen who use the floor of their bedroom as a horizontal closet.

When to Employ: When there are at least two distinct layers of clothing covering the bedroom floor.

What You'll Need: Dirty clothes and siblings with a keen sense of revenge.

Amanda was your basic surfer girl. She was fourteen, enthralled with boys who surfed, didn't much care for school, and excelled at any sport you can think of. She had the surfer girl look down pat—long sun-streaked hair, a tan, big smile with braces, hemp bracelets and anklets. She considered her parents to be, in her terms, "beyond lame" and "clueless," regardless of the fact that it was their hard work that allowed her to have the cool clothes and surfboard and all the accoutrements of the surfer girl lifestyle.

Here's the rub: Amanda had the habit of leaving all those hard-earned clothes (dirty and clean, all mixed together) in a jumble on the floor. According to her parents, she had taken sloppiness to a new level. They joked that it had been months, if not years, since she had actually seen her floor and claimed she would be unable to remember what color her carpeting was, or even if she had carpeting. She was ankle-deep in shoes, jeans, tops, sweatshirts, damp towels, smelly socks, and so on, and all attempts to get her to use her dresser, and closet, and laundry hamper, had failed.

Her dad admitted he had given up even trying to get Amanda to clean her room, because he was worn out from all of her arguing. He had begun to say things like, "What the hell, it's her room, let her keep it like a pigpen if that's what she wants." Her mom held fast to the notion that teens should be allowed some level of sloppiness for sure, but no one was going to leave her home without having been raised to live like a civilized human being. She had a friend whose son had been asked by his college roommates to move out because of his sloppy ways, and she did not want this to happen to Amanda one day.

When I met with Amanda and her parents, I asked her how she felt about meeting with me to talk about the state of her room. She looked at me, rolled her eyes, and gave me one of those answers teenagers use when they don't want to be bothered:

"What-ev-er."

I listened as her parents explained their frustration over the way she kept her room, and then I commented to Amanda that since it didn't seem to bother her that her floor was covered with clothes, even dirty clothes, one option would be for the whole family to just throw their dirty clothes into her room. I said it was a perfect solution for everyone because her room could *easily* hold several weeks' worth of dirty clothes for the entire family and her mom wouldn't have to empty the laundry hamper so often. I continued to explain that from now on, whenever anyone in the family took off any article of dirty clothing (other than underwear, of course—this program was meant to get her attention, not to gross her out) they were to just toss it into her room. Dirty socks, dirty T-shirts, dirty jeans, sweats, you name it—into her room they would go. I should mention that her dad was huge—about six feet five and 275 pounds. He worked outside in the heat and by the time he got home on summer nights his socks and his T-shirt (about the size of a flag) were, shall we say, moderately *odiferous.*

Her response was total disbelief that her parents would go this far. When they assured her they would unless she decided to get her room into more reasonable shape, she upped the ante: she told them she didn't care what they did. They could use any stupid method they wanted, she said, and it wouldn't bother her, not one bit.

Given that Amanda drew such a line in the sand, her parents had to follow through. They refused to argue with her about whether it was fair and refused to back down when she told them her friends would think they were bad parents: "Oh, don't worry, dear. You've already assured us that *all* your friends leave their rooms messy. In fact, you've always told us that your room is *clean* compared to theirs. So they won't even notice your room is a little bit messier than usual when they come over to visit."

It took only a few days before Amanda caved in and decided to clean up. But what's more important is that the vast majority of kids who hear her story decide pretty quickly to put more effort into getting their rooms in better shape so they can avoid a similar fate.

In reading about Amanda, you probably noticed we did several things you should also do when you use interventions from the Box of Tricks. First, we told her exactly what we intended to do. Second, we gave her an out, that soft landing we talked about earlier, indicating that her parents would not have to do anything at all if she made reasonable changes and made them quickly.

Third, her parents used a proper sense of proportion once they had to follow through. They didn't actually flood her with a torrent of dirty clothes, just a few items here and there every day. This brought an end to a problem the family had been arguing about for literally years. Even Amanda learned to laugh about this episode. Another plus: her eight-year-old brother learned a lesson from watching what happened to her and, as far as I know, did not experience the same fate.

Trick: The Victim of Capitalism

Use It On: Children eight to fourteen whose aggregate value of all toys combined exceeds the aggregate value of all your toys combined.

When to Employ: When the little princes and princesses can't seem to keep any of those many, many toys where they belong.

What You'll Need: Cardboard boxes; attic or secure closet.

What parent doesn't enjoy giving his or her children toys and watching their little faces light up? But what parent hasn't also been held hostage at the grocery store or the mall or some big toy store and bought his child something he didn't need any more than he needed a sixth finger, just to avoid a fit or a public confrontation? The end result too often is that your child ends up with enough toys to open his own toy store, but fails to figure out how to actually put any of them away.

One family I worked with provides a case in point. Both parents had grown up on farms in rural North Carolina. Successful school administrators, they freely admitted they had succumbed to the desire to give their ten-year-old son, Spence, more than they had as children. Spence's mom had tried everything to keep his toys organized. She had set up his room with bins that had labels on them. One for cars, one for balls, one for video games, and so on. But he preferred to just keep everything dumped out on the floor. Half of what he had was broken from being stepped on, and his parents groused that he didn't understand the value of anything they worked so hard to provide.

I met with Spence's parents briefly before I brought him in, and we cooked up a strategy. His parents were to tell him they owed him a huge apology because they had turned him into a victim of capitalism. This is how they explained it: "Sweetheart, we are so sorry. We've worked so hard and have become so successful that we bought you more than you could ever possibly manage. How could any child be expected to take care of so much *stuff*?"

They then went on to explain that the only way to relieve him of the huge burden they had placed on him was to box up half of his stuff over the next few days and put it into storage so he would no longer have to deal with it. Spence looked at them like they were space aliens who had kidnapped his real mom and dad.

As he continued to stare at them with a confused look on his face, they explained that because this was one big, happy experiment, in two weeks if he still couldn't keep his room straight, they would come to him with another apology. It would be clear that even *half* of all the stuff they had given him was still too much to cope with. They would then box up half of that half and place it into storage also and so on and so on until there were only a few things left—a couple of balls, a few Legos, one video game, perhaps—the point being that they just knew sooner or later they would find the level where he could manage his stuff and keep things neat.

This is how they finished the talk with him: "You know, we could be wrong. If you get your room cleaned up in the next day or two and keep it clean, we'll have to admit that we were totally wrong about this and we won't have to do the experiment. And you know we sure do hate to admit we're wrong!"

As with any of the interventions we'll cover, if you use the Victim of Capitalism at your house, you *must* be willing to follow through. What you are really hoping for is that your child, like Spence, will hear your intent and decide to clean up before you actually have to follow through on your crazy idea. However, one thing I have heard on many occasions is that parents begin to understand that they really *have* burdened a child with so much junk that he truly can't keep it organized, and a good pruning of the clutter actually works wonders.

Trick: Fashion Feng Shui

Use It On: Victims of fashion capitalism.

When to Employ: When you can't walk through your child's room without getting shirts or tops or pants or skirts wrapped around your ankles.

What You'll Need: A good supply of boxes and some Eastern sensibilities.

Here's a variation of the Victim of Capitalism trick that you can consider using when you're tired of wading through all the clothes on your child's floor. Tell her you've decided to institute the ancient principle of Fashion Feng Shui, in which the wise person comes to a realization that too much fashion clutter leaves a person's life feeling cluttered. In order to protect her from this, you intend to box up all of her clothes except three pairs of jeans, five shirts, two pairs of shoes, and enough socks and underwear for a week. Explain that such a reduction should make it quite easy for her to keep her room looking neat and harmonious, thus allowing all of her internal energy sources to align in a manner that induces peace and harmony. Of course, she always has the option to just hang her stuff up, which would pretty much force you to keep your energy meridians to yourself.

Trick: Would You Like Me to Pick That Up for You?

Use It On: Children six to twelve who seem to think the trafficked areas and hallways of your house are their own personal storage lanes.

When to Employ: When you try to walk between your sofa and coffee table and stumble over your kid's book bag again.

What You'll Need: Trash bags in large quantity (not the see-through kind!).

This is another technique to use if your child leaves her things strewn throughout your house. Tell her that you are willing to pick up anything she leaves on the floor in the common areas of your house (living room, den, kitchen, hallways, and so on). Tell her that you will put whatever you pick up—clothes, shoes, coats, books, homework, music players, CDs, and so on—in a trash bag, and that you will store the trash bag somewhere in your garage, or basement, or storage closet. Indicate that you will use a different trash bag each day. Be sure to explain that because you are so busy, you will not be likely to remember exactly which bag you put any particular item into, or where you put any of the bags. So, if there is something specific that she's looking for, she will just have to go search the house for all the bags until she finds it. Be sure to explain that it will be much better for her to simply get into the habit of picking her stuff up so you won't have to use this technique.

Trick: Clean Laundry

Use It On: Laundry ingrates, ages ten to fourteen.

When to Employ: When everything you've carefully washed and folded ends up on the floor.

What You'll Need: Clean laundry, preferably after it has been sitting in the dryer for a while and is good and wrinkly because your ingrate doesn't seem to mind wrinkles.

I've talked to many, many frustrated moms who go to the trouble to wash their child's laundry, fold it, and put it on her bed, asking only that she put it away neatly. Instead, it ends up on the floor, stepped on, wrinkled, and strewn all over the place.

If this is the case at your house, warn your child that unless she starts taking better care of her clothes, you will take the next big load out of the dryer in a balled-up lump and just plop it on the floor at the foot of her bed. When she protests that this is not *fair*, as she is bound to, tell her this is precisely where her clothes end up anyway, so she should thank you for saving her the time and effort.

If she says she doesn't believe you will actually go this far, it becomes your job to convince her you will. If she insists she really, really doesn't believe you, this will tell you that you have created an atmosphere in your home in which your child does not think you're willing to make her uncomfortable in any way. Your options are to back off, which proves to her you're a toothless tiger, or to go ahead and give her a taste of the trick so she knows you aren't bluffing. If after all this she still says she doesn't care, you then need to seriously consider teaching her how to do her own laundry. Chances are she'll soon begin taking better care of her clean clothes.

And now for the queen mother of all tricks related to a messy bedroom . . .

Trick: Grounded from Your Room

Use It On: Children ten to fourteen who have been yelled at for at least one year about how crummy their rooms look but have done absolutely zip to improve things.

When to Employ: Prior to the fraying of your very last nerve.

What You'll Need: A bedroom that your child sleeps in and believes to be his, or hers, and a clear-headed enough viewpoint to realize that the room actually belongs to *you*, given that you're the one who pays the bills. You're going to also need some tape, a Magic Marker, and some blank paper to make a sign.

Everybody knows about being grounded *to* your room, but have you ever thought about being grounded *from* your room? I suggest parents consider this for children who love hanging out in their rooms but who also refuse to keep them up to human standards.

This is what you do: first, warn your child you intend to use this trick if he or she does not make changes in how the bedroom is kept. Be sure to explain it thoroughly, because it comes with very real consequences.

If your child continues to ignore you and you have finally reached your limit, tape a sign on the door that reads CONDEMNED! ROOM UNFIT FOR HUMAN HABITATION! When your child gets home and flips out, calmly explain it like this: "I warned you about this, did I not? However, you continued to keep your room wrecked, so now you will be grounded from it for five days." Explain to your child that he or she will not be allowed into the room for any reason other than to spend time cleaning it or to get clothes for the day. Tell your child that while the room is condemned, he or she will have to get out a sleeping bag or some covers and sleep on a couch or on a carpeted floor. As with all of the tricks, explain that you don't really want to do this to him or her, but you will if your request for a civilized state of affairs continues to be ignored.

I've explained this technique to many children and their parents over the years. Invariably, the kids are outraged about it at first, and the parents love it. A trick like this has a way of rebalancing the family power structure. It reminds the child, regardless of age, that his or her ownership of the room is an illusion. Do kids begin to keep their room in an obsessively clean fashion after hearing all of this? No, and they shouldn't. However, it establishes the fact that while they will be given leeway to be kids, tweens, and teens, there are limits to what is acceptable.

Trick: Alien Watch

Use It On: Children age eight to ten (or so) who like science fiction and who seem incapable of admitting that they are the ones who left the plates of chips and cheese or the half-empty soda cans or the candy wrappers strewn throughout your house.

When to Employ: Once you're truly sick of all the litter and trash, because this one might take several days.

What You'll Need: One straight-backed chair for each child. It will also be helpful if your family is familiar with *Star Trek* and understands the phrase "Beam me up."

Here's one way for parents to explain to their children that they are considering using Alien Watch: "Since neither of you is willing to admit you left trash in the den, it is obvious what is happening. Space aliens have detected the snack foods we keep in our house and when we're not watching, they beam down and have a party! When they hear us coming, they signal the mother ship to beam them up before we can even get a glimpse of them. Fortunately, we have figured out a way to capture them."

(As usual, be prepared for your kids to look at you and go "Huh?" Just keep explaining.)

"The aliens have motion sensors in their noses and will not beam down if they register any movement or sound at all in the kitchen. So, you will have to sit perfectly still in a straight-backed chair in the kitchen. You'll also have to remain perfectly quiet. Then, when the aliens beam down and materialize, you leap out of your chair and tackle them! We are going to have you go on alien watch for one hour each night until we get this problem solved. Do you understand?"

When your kids object, as surely they will, go on to explain that the aliens are probably listening to the conversation with their scanning devices, and if they are smart they have already realized it is no longer safe to have parties at your house. Tell your kids that if suddenly there's no more trash being left all over your house, that will be all the proof you need that the aliens have bugged out, and there will be no need for anyone to go on alien watch.

Trick: Channel Changer Wars

Use It On: Children age six to fourteen who seem intent on leaving the television remote control under the couch, in the kitchen, or out in the garage.

When to Employ: On the increasingly rare occasion that there's something worth watching on television, but your remote is nowhere to be found.

What You'll Need: Lots of good hiding places.

Have you asked your kids to please, please, *please* be more careful about where they leave the television remote control, only to be unable to locate it once you're ready for some zoning out yourself? One mom (this is absolutely true) looked up and down for her remote, only later to find it in the freezer. Here's the fix: hide the remote in a place only you know about. Go get it whenever you want to watch TV. If your kids ask you where you found it, make up some location: under the sofa, in a drawer, and so on. Then, when you finish using it, hide it again. It won't necessarily hurt your kids to miss television for a few days. If they figure out how to turn the TV on without the remote, it also won't hurt them to get a little exercise by having to get up and down to go change the channel by hand. After a few days, have the remote reappear, and sit down with your kids to talk about the importance of having one area it generally stays in. If it stays put after that, fine. If not, your biggest challenge will be to remember where *you* left it.

Trick: Dishwasher Practice

Use It On: Kids from six to fourteen who don't particularly care that you want them to put their dirty dishes in the dishwasher.

When to Employ: The day it finally dawns on you that your children don't particularly care that you want them to put their dirty dishes in the dishwasher.

What You'll Need: This one's simple. Your kids will provide you with all the dirty dishes you'll need.

There's a way to deal with children who won't clean up their dirty dishes. You know the type of child I'm talking about. She manages to put her dirty dish on the countertop *above* the dishwasher, but never quite manages to get it *in* the dishwasher.

Perhaps you should return to a proven technique: repetition, as seen earlier in our research on door slammers. Tell her the next time she fails to put her dirty dish in the dishwasher, you will apologize for not having taught her how to properly use the dishwasher. After this, you'll ask her to come into the kitchen for practice. You'll have her put the dirty dish in, and then remove it so that she can put it back in again. She can do this over and over for about ten minutes. Soon, she will get quite good at putting dishes in the dishwasher. Of course, if after practicing it turns out over the next few days that she still can't quite get her dishes in the dishwasher, you will have to apologize to her again and tell her that you obviously underestimated how much practice she actually needed. So, the next practice session will be fifteen minutes. If for some odd reason she *still* doesn't get it, she will need to be placed in charge of the whole family's dirty dishes, night after night, until she gets the knack, which might not be a bad idea to begin with. Whatever happened to that old concept called chores, anyway?

Trick: Pretend It's a Picnic

Use It On: Kids six to fourteen who earn a grade of C or below on dishwasher practice.

When to Employ: After it's apparent that your child does not have sufficient energy, motivation, or coordination to put a plate in the dishwasher.

What You'll Need: Paper plates, plastic forks, spoons, and knives. A red and white checkerboard tablecloth is optional.

This one is simple enough. If your child flunks dishwasher practice, tell him to get in the car with you so that you can go get some supplies. This is when you let it be known that anyone in your household who cannot manage to get his plate to where it ought to go after a meal will now have the convenience of drinking from paper cups, eating off of paper plates, and using plastic silverware. He'll have to deal with the cheapest items available, the ones where the food soaks through the bottom of the plate, the cups only hold a small amount of liquid, and the forks and spoons crack. Remind your child that should he fail in his attempt to deposit his used paper plate and plastic accoutrements into the trash can, you'll be more than happy to supervise practicing this important life skill. If your child carps about any of this, tell him to pretend it's a picnic.

LIARS, FIBBERS, AND SCAMMERS

All children lie. The only difference among them comes in frequency and degree. Some children give lying an occasional try and stick to the proverbial "white lies." Others lie constantly—the more important the subject matter, the more likely that the truth will never cross their lips. The reason they lie? Typically, they're attempting to escape punishment. ("I really, really, really did hand in my homework. It's not my fault that my teacher lost my last six assignments.") Sometimes they're trying to scam you so you won't figure out what they're actually up to. ("I'm going out with, uh, Stephen. He's from a very nice family. His dad used to be the pope, or something like that.") And then there's the preemptive lie. ("I knew you wouldn't let me go, so I lied to you about where I'd be.") If your child takes lying too far, to the point where it is both constant and without remorse, you're best advised to seek professional help. Lying can be the leading edge of a number of behavior disorders, as well as an indicator of depression or anxiety. However, if it strikes you that your child is a garden-variety scam artist, you should keep on reading in an attempt to pull him back from the brink.

Trick: The Liar's Program

Use It On: Liars, fibbers, and scammers, age six through fourteen.

When to Employ: Once it is obvious that your child has a learning disability when it comes to telling the truth.

What You'll Need: Cleaning supplies and other household-chore essentials (vacuum cleaners, scrub brushes, rakes, brooms, mops, hedge clippers, etc.).

Do you have a child who lies to you frequently? If so, you have probably talked yourself blue in the face, using reason, logic, and morality all to no avail. If your child seems intent on lying, you should consider telling him about the Liar's Program. Here's how it might go:

Parent: "I'm thinking about using the Liar's Program with you. You've gotten so good at lying that I can't tell when you're doing it and when you're not. So I'm just going to assume that if your lips are moving, you're lying.

"I'm going to show you what it will be like to be on the Liar's Program. We're going to pretend it's Saturday morning. I'll wake you up at 7 in the morning so you have time to get cleaned up and dressed. I'll make breakfast for you at 7:30. Starting at 8, the rest of your day will be split into one-hour units. Now we're going to role-play."

Child: "This is stupid."

Parent: "You are precisely right. We should not have to deal with lying in this house, but since we do, we're going to do something about it. Now, it's Saturday morning and I want to know what you would like for breakfast."

Child: "Uh, OK. I'd like pancakes and bacon."

Parent: "I don't believe you. I don't think you really like pancakes and bacon at all. Please tell me what you would really like for breakfast."

Child: "What? I told you I want pancakes and bacon."

Parent: "And I told you I don't believe you because you lie about *everything*!"

Child: "I want cereal, then."

Parent: "I still don't believe you. Since you won't tell me the truth, I'm just going to fix you a bowl of grits and a glass of milk."

Child: "No, that stuff is gross."

Parent: "Sorry, it's grits or nothing."

After breakfast is finished:

Parent: "What would you like to do between 8 and 9?"

Child: "Watch cartoons."

Parent: "No, that's not the truth."

Child: "I told you, cartoons! I love cartoons!"

Parent: "Nope, don't believe you. Since you won't tell me the truth, I'll have to figure out something for you to do. OK, I've got it. You can rake all the leaves out of the flower beds. That ought to take you about an hour. Now, get to work."

This is how the morning will go. Every hour you'll meet with your child and ask him what he wants to do during that hour. You will steadfastly disbelieve anything he says, and end up giving him more chores, such as scrubbing toilets, tubs, and bathroom sinks, cleaning out the litter box, or vacuuming all the carpets and rugs. If he tries to get tricky with you and tells you he wants to do chores, feel free to say "Thank you," and tell him his wish just came true.

Remind him that lunch will be particularly interesting because you will not be willing to believe he would really like a sandwich or a sub or a pizza. What you believe he really wants is a plain can of tuna with a slice of bread and a glass of milk. Remind him also that after lunch, the rest of the day will also be split into one-hour units. Tell him the Liar's Program will be over at dinner, at which time you will sit and have a good meal along with a discussion on whether he intends to stop the lying. If he does not, the Liar's Program can become a Saturday staple.

How do kids respond to the Liar's Program? The number of kids who've actually had to go on it is small because just hearing about it and going through the role-play is enough to make most of them do a U-turn.

Trick: The Liar's Program Lite

Use It On: Those same fibbers, age six to fourteen.

When to Employ: When you want to get your point across about lying, but you don't have time for the day-long version of the Liar's Program.

What You'll Need: Ask your child what he or she wants. That's all you need to know to make the Lite version work.

To use this trick, simply tell your child in a matter-of-fact way that you have come to believe everything she says is a lie, and experience has taught you that you cannot trust anything she says. Then act as if the discussion is over (she will be relieved).

Later, casually ask her what she would like for dinner. Suppose she says lasagna with Italian bread. Say OK. Then fix something you know she will not particularly like—meatloaf, perhaps. When she protests, point out that you thought she was lying about the lasagna, given that she lies about everything else.

Tell her if she continues to lie, she should not be surprised when she ends up at the grocery store after asking you to take her to her friend's house. Your explanation will be the same each time: "Sorry. Thought you were lying about wanting to go to Kate's."

ARGUERS

"I am not young enough to know everything."
—*Oscar Wilde, nineteenth-century*
Irish poet and writer

Every adult claims to have never argued with their parents the way their own children now argue with them. Could this possibly be true? Just think about a three-generation family I consulted with. The grandmother said to the mother of the highly argumentative granddaughter, "I warned you one day you'd have a child who'd give you a taste of what you gave me. Sweeeet!"

That said, arguing certainly seems like a serious problem in our culture. Too many parents tell me *they* want to run away from home. Almost every high school teacher I know can't wait to retire because of the corrosive disrespect they encounter daily in the classroom. I frequently work with teenagers who've been fired from one fast-food job after another because it's yet to occur to them that their supervisors can indeed tell them what to do. Fight the power, as they say! With this in mind, you might be interested in some techniques that can greatly decrease the amount of arguing that goes on in your home.

Trick: The Arguing Program

Use It On: Your future attorney, age eight to fourteen.

When to Employ: Once you realize you cannot tell your child that in most parts of the known universe, spheres are round, without getting pushback.

What You'll Need: Having read some movie reviews would be helpful.

I've got to tell you about Roger, a very bright and argumentative ten-year-old. The best way to describe him is like this: regardless of what you wanted him to do, he would start his rebuttal (he always had a rebuttal) with the word "unfortunately." Here's the twist: Roger was one of those kids who, in the search to find his own identity, had borrowed the mannerisms of a movie character. He'd say "unfortunately" very much like the late Heath Ledger, who played the Joker so brilliantly in *The Dark Knight*: "Un-for-tu-nut-*leeee*," drawing out the last syllable. Ask him to take out the trash? "Un-for-tu-nut-*leeee*, that is not high on my list of priorities, Mother. I happen to be busy with other things." You can imagine how happy his mother was with this.

If you have a Roger (or a Rogette)—someone who argues with you at every turn—you've probably already anticipated where we are headed. Here we return once again to the idea of giving a child a taste of his own medicine. In this version, you warn your child that you're going to argue with him throughout the day, over totally senseless issues, just so he can see what it's like to live with him. Here's a sample of what I told Roger's mom to do:

Roger: "Is it OK if I go to the movies tonight with Joe and Jerelle?"

Mom: "What's playing?"

Roger: "That new cartoon movie about aliens from Mars."

Mom: "What's the rating?"

Roger: "It's rated G, Mom. Joe's dad is taking us."

Mom: "I can't understand why you never wanted me to take you to see *Twilight*. That was such a popular movie with kids your age."

Roger: "Mom, that's a girl movie."

Mom: "Well, there's certainly nothing wrong with going to a girl movie. You might learn something about how to talk about your feelings."

Roger: "Mom! I don't want to go see some girl movie about feelings! I want to see guy movies."

Mom: "But it would give you something to talk to the girls about. There's nothing wrong with that. There certainly won't be any girls at your space alien movie. Girls like boys who can talk to them about what they like."

Roger: "I just want to go to the alien movie! Sheesh!"

And so on.

If you use this technique, at some point you'll smile at your child and ask him what it was like to be pulled into an argument over something pointless. Often your child will act like it hasn't made a dent, but if done frequently enough, you will see some changes. And sometimes a little change is all a weary parent needs.

Trick: The Compliment:
A Degree in Arguology

Use It On: Your young lawyer, age eight to twelve.

When to Employ: When you want to use a paradoxical approach in hopes of channeling your child's argumentative side in the right direction.

What You'll Need: A Web connection to get to documentic.com, or similar sites.

Come again? When you want to do *what*? Here's the deal: it's easy to argue with your child about her arguing. But what if you want to actually see the positive side of her basic nature, and compliment her on her skills? A compliment will disarm her faster than you might imagine in the midst of an argument, and she won't know what to do when you whack her with a friendly attitude about an aspect of her personality that always seems to be a point of contention.

Child: "I don't see why I can't go across Main Street by myself. It's not like it's a freeway or something. I know how to look both ways and not go running out into traffic. I'm ten years old! I'm not a baby."

Mom: "No good mom's going to let her ten-year-old cross that street alone. It's way too busy."

Child: "But you've taught me to go across streets alone, and I always stop and look both ways, and I know to look for how fast a car is going. And whether the driver is driving crazy or not."

Mom: "Well, the answer is still no. But I really need to compliment you on how well you do when you're arguing your position. You use really good language and logic. I'm very impressed."

I had a similar talk with a girl at my office. She started out in a highly adversarial manner, obviously trying to defeat me. By the time I finished complimenting her on her strong use of reason and logic, she was much more reasonable and enjoyable to talk to. As a reward, I went to documentic.com and printed her out a nice certificate in beautiful gothic script. It showed that she had been granted the degree of Juris Doctorate in Arguology, *with distinction*, from the Virginia College of Law. She was very taken aback at first, but indicated that she actually did think she was good at arguing her side of an issue and would make a good lawyer.

Print something similar for your young lawyer. And next time she takes you to the wall, remember to compliment her on her verbal skills. Chances are it will make things go just a tad better.

Trick: The Equality Program

Use It On: Tweens and teens who confuse being as tall as you with being your equal.

When to Employ: When shooting up in height coincides with shooting off at the mouth.

What You'll Need: A child in the midst of a growth spurt.

For whatever reason, when some kids get to be roughly as tall as their moms, they assume they've reached equality in the family power structure. That's when they take arguing to a new height (no pun intended). As one kid said to his mom at my office, "If you can ground me, why can't I ground you?"

The next time your child tries to argue with you about who's who and what's what in your family system, sit her down and thank her profusely:

You: "Thank you!"

Child, eyeing you warily: "What are you talking about?"

You: "Since you seem to believe that you're now my equal, I'm going to give you a promotion. It will mean much, much more responsibility around the house—grown-up type of responsibility. But apparently that's what you want. So this is where we can start: I'm going to turn over half of my duties to you, in particular the ones you're always complaining that I do so poorly. Cooking . . . cleaning . . . laundry . . ."

Child: "But that's not, that's not . . ."

Be prepared for a confused or flabbergasted look on your child's face. For once her mouth will move but no sound will come out! Once she thinks you're going to give her some real equality, she'll stop complaining and back off quickly.

Trick: The Real Meaning of "OK"

Use It On: Yourself!

When to Employ: When your kids don't seem to pay any attention to what you tell them to do. In just a moment you'll understand why.

What You'll Need: The ability to exclude the word "OK" from your vocabulary.

This is a very small trick, given that it involves only one word. Here's the deal: if you end your sentences with "OK" when you're talking to a stubborn child, knock it off immediately. While you probably think you're making sure he understands, he'll think you're seeking his permission or agreement.

Example: "Tomorrow morning I want you to clean up your room. If you don't, I'm going to have to take away your video game for the whole day. OK?" You can pretty much predict how well this is going to work.

STICKY FINGERS

"For those who take, but do not earn,
must pay most dearly in their turn."

—*J. K. Rowling,* Harry Potter and the Sorcerer's Stone

Some kids borrow, and some kids steal. It can be difficult to tell them apart because the only thing you know for sure is that your belongings end up in their possession without your permission. Borrowers don't intend to keep what they've borrowed. They just want to use it and put it back, although many of them have the bad habit of putting things back broken or dirty or damaged in some way.

Stealers, on the other hand, believe what they've stolen now belongs to them, and will go to great lengths to protect their new possessions. One of their favorite things is to hide what they've stolen in places not directly associated with them. One boy I knew hid his stolen goods in his sister's room!

You don't have to worry too much about borrowers. They'll probably grow out of it. Worry about the ones who consistently plan their capers well in advance, are stealing increasingly valuable things, and lie as coolly as the proverbial cucumber when caught. They may need professional help. All the others should respond well to the tricks you're about to learn.

Trick: Hide the Tennis Shoe

Use It On: Kids eight to twelve who borrow your stuff but tend to lose it.

When to Employ: After you're tired of your iPod being gone for days on end because your kid admits to having taken it, but can't remember where he put it.

What You'll Need: The ability to hide things creatively.

OK, a little info about the history of tricks: Hide the Tennis Shoe was really the very first trick I ever invented. I just didn't realize at the time that it was a trick. It was prompted by my work with a sunny-faced, mop-haired eleven-year-old who was driving his mom nuts by borrowing her things and losing them. To put this into historical context, this was way before there were iPods and laptops and smart phones loaded with games and movies that kids today borrow and lose. This was back in the day when fancy tennis shoes had just hit the market and were all the rage, and Nike Inc. was beginning its ascendency. We're talking *1980*.

The things he borrowed, and invariably misplaced, were things like her handheld calculator, or her Sony Walkman, or the keys to her car because he liked to sit in it and listen to her tape player. I tried every counseling technique I could think of to get him to change. I tried reward-based techniques, punishment-based techniques, cognitive techniques, on and on and on. Finally, out of sheer frustration, I warned him that if he didn't knock it off with his borrowing and losing, he might notice that something of his own had disappeared.

Here's the conversation I had with him, as best as I can recall:

Me: "If you don't stop taking your mother's things, something of yours will have to go missing to give you a taste of how frustrated you make her feel."

Him: "Hey, that wouldn't be fair!"

Me: "Fair? You lost her car keys again last Saturday."

Him: "Well, I found them."

Me: "*She* found them. On Sunday."

Him: "It's not my fault she doesn't have a spare key."

Me: "If I'm correct, *you* lost it."

Him: "Oh."

Me: "So if you take any more of her stuff, she's going to hide one of your tennis shoes."

Him: "But I'll know it was her because I'm sitting right here listening to you tell her to do it."

Me: "That doesn't matter. If you say to her, 'Dr. Riley told you to hide my tennis shoe,' she will say back to you, 'Darling, Dr. Riley would never tell a parent to do such a thing.'"

And that's how it went. The next time something of hers went missing, she hid one of his tennis shoes for a day. He frantically looked high and low for it before having to put on his church shoes and get on out to the bus stop. Then, at the end of the day, he found his shoe beside the toilet, "Right," as his mother said, "where you must have left it."

His response: "Arrrrgh!"

Some good things certainly came out of this intervention: he stopped borrowing without permission, and made a huge effort to put things back where they belonged once he had finished using them. His mother made it clear that if he borrowed her stuff and managed to break it or damage it by being careless, his tennis shoe would definitely come back with no laces, or the laces tied in so many tight little knots that he'd never get them out. Today's version of this? Return your child's iPod with the earbuds missing (let them show up in a day or two) or the cords knotted up.

Finally, his mother remembered to have a spare key made for her car, and hid it where he could never, ever find it.

Trick: You Need More Stuff

Use It On: Kids eight to twelve who can't resist sneaking into your room and borrowing your stuff.

When to Employ: Once you know the following rule to be true: the more expensive the item, the greater the chance you'll find it in your child's room.

What You'll Need: Lots of extra stuff that you need to store somewhere.

What do you do when your child keeps taking your things without permission? You've tried every moral and legal argument you can think of to get her to stop, and nothing is working. You sit down with her and explain that she obviously has a deep-seated, secret desire to have more stuff for her room. Let her know that you will help, and that you have a proven method. You intend to move all of your extra outdated or out-of-season shoes and clothes into her room, as well as some of her dad's old stuff, and maybe even some extra furniture you're not using. Example:

Parent: "Every time I turn around, I'm finding my things in your room, and you never even asked to use them. Basically, if my things are missing, I know where to go to find them."

Child: "Sor-ree!"

Parent: "That's *not* a decent apology, and you know it. I think there's a deeper issue going on. I think way down inside you don't believe you have enough stuff for your room. So you take everybody else's stuff and put it in there."

Child: "No, I don't think like that. I just forget to put stuff back after I use it."

Parent: "I don't think so. It happens too often. So I've decided to help you. I'm going to put more stuff into your room. I've got a ton of winter clothes I'm not using right now, boxes of books up in the attic, your dad's got about a zillion outdated ties. We're going to make sure you feel like you have enough stuff in your room to keep you satisfied and happy."

Child: "Mom!"

That's what I did briefly with an eleven-year-old I worked with. Usually what she borrowed was something belonging to her mom, like a lipstick or other makeup. But occasionally it was something larger. She had actually been found wearing her mom's diamond necklace to school. Her brother's MP3 player and headphones were not safe as long as she was around, either.

Her parents held fast to their argument and told her that over the next few days she might find her room filling up with all kinds of stuff if she didn't cease raiding their bedroom and her brother's room. They pointed out that she had lots of empty space in her bookcase, and that the tops of her dressers could be used for stacking things one on top of the other.

She did OK for about a week, but then her mother began to notice items were missing again. With no further warning, her parents began to transfer several boxes of old dishes into her room and placed them neatly on her dresser. She howled like any angry, aggrieved tweener will, but her parents stuck hard to the original explanation that she secretly desired more stuff.

It didn't take long for this girl to learn the valuable lesson that if she simply asked permission to use other people's things, and if she used them respectfully and put them back where she found them, they would be more than happy to let her borrow.

Trick: Guard Duty

Use It On: Kids eight to twelve who steal, but won't admit it even if they've been caught red-handed.

When to Employ: When so much of your stuff has been stolen that you're considering a trip to the hardware store to buy dead-bolts.

What You'll Need: A nice boring hallway.

My next patient, twelve-year-old Toby, was on his way to becoming a stealer rather than a borrower. His father told me that he was seriously considering putting deadbolts on everyone's bedroom doors because no one could trust Toby anymore. Toby was taking collector cards from his older brother's room to trade or sell at school. His father knew he used the money to buy candy, gum, or soft drinks, because the leftovers from his purchases were scattered throughout his room—there were candy wrappers and Mountain Dew bottles all over the place. Toby steadfastly denied stealing anything from anyone, despite the fact that he had no known source of income. He insisted repeatedly that his friends *gave* him the candy and the drinks—*for free.*

Then, when a twenty-dollar bill went missing from his sister's room, Toby swore up and down that he had nothing to do with it, even when it was later found in his pants pocket. His family stood aghast as he went on a rant about how he had no idea in the world how it got there—and then he did the unthinkable, he actually accused his sister of putting it there to get him in trouble. Fortunately, and to his credit, Toby realized almost immediately that he had gone too far and he broke down crying. "This is when we realized that he still had a conscience," his parents said. "We knew there was a sweet kid in there, even though he couldn't bring himself to actually admit what he was doing."

I gave Toby several choices. First, since he always insisted he had not stolen anything, I told him that we would take him at his word. However, that still left a significant problem: someone, or some*thing*, was getting into the house and taking people's stuff, and it was probably this unknown person, or *thing*, who was leaving soda bottles and candy wrappers on his floor as well. Because of this invasion, Toby was going to be placed in charge of security. I told him his job would be to spend his spare time in the hallway that led to his mother's room, his room, and his brother's and sister's rooms. He was to make sure no one, or no *thing*, snuck into the rooms and took stuff. I assured him it would be perfectly acceptable to take a chair into the hallway, because he would be there for long stretches of time on evenings and weekends and would probably get tired of standing.

As always, I provided Toby with an out by saying that if things just suddenly stopped disappearing somehow, he could resume a normal kid life. Instead of having to spend hours guarding the hallway, he could spend his spare time playing, reading, hanging out with friends, and so on. We also discussed the idea that if the stealing stopped, his parents would find ways for him to earn some allowance money so that he could buy the candy and drinks and video games he wanted.

Toby ended up standing Guard Duty at the entrance to the hallway on several Saturdays. His parents had him do it for an hour at a time, once in the morning, once in the afternoon, and once in the evening. He was highly resistant, and muttered loud and long that it was the dumbest thing he had ever had to do, that his parents were being mean to him, and so on. His parents insisted just as vocally that it was no less dumb than sneaking into his brother's room and taking baseball cards or magic cards.

Getting a significant taste of Guard Duty ultimately did him a world of good. His parents made it exceptionally clear that they would have him stand Guard Duty on an as-needed basis, as in *needed* anytime anyone in the family realized that something was missing. It took awhile, but when he finally came out with his admissions and apologies they seemed genuine enough to get his parents to back off.

Trick: I Don't Know Where That Came From

Use It On: Kids eight to fourteen, who, although clearly in possession of stolen stuff, conveniently can't remember where they got it, whom it really belongs to, or how long they've had it.

When to Employ: When it's obviously necessary to jog your child's memory but you've come to the conclusion that car batteries and jumper cables are not the way to go.

What You'll Need: Your sticky-fingered son or daughter will provide the stolen stuff.

Here's another technique you can use if you discover your child has some valuable new gizmo that you know you didn't give him, and all signs point to the idea that he got it via the five-finger discount. When you ask him, however, where he got it, he gives you some thoroughly convincing answer like "A kid on the bus gave it to me," or "I found it."

First, do not accept the answer "I found it." If your child insists this is the truth, tell him you will be happy to take him to the police department, where he can turn in the found merchandise and describe to a police sergeant exactly where it was found. If he tells you he cannot remember the exact spot, tell him that "close" will be good enough. This will usually bring out a more realistic answer, such as "Joe gave it to me," or "I paid Bobby five dollars for it." At least with these answers you can ask to speak to Joe or Bobby or their parent in order to get confirmation. Until, that is, your child insists he does not know Joe's or Bobby's last name, phone number, or address. This is when you say, "No worries. I will go with you to school tomorrow and we will bring this up with the principal. I'm sure he will know who you're talking about." Somewhere in there, the truth will come spilling out.

But suppose your child takes the more risky ploy of simply saying to you, "I can't remember where I got it." This is what one thirteen-year-old, Jack, told his parents when they wanted to know where he got the iPod he was listening to.

I told Jack it clearly might be difficult to remember where every object he owned came from. However, with time and concentration, it also might be possible to jog his memory. In order to do this, we would have him follow a particular procedure: every night, his mother or father would put the iPod on the kitchen table, and he would have to sit and stare at it for one hour in hopes that concentrating on nothing else would bring back the memory of where he got it. His parents would be willing to do this until he recovered his memory. They told him it would be best not to make any plans for evenings or weekends because he had to be home when his mom or dad were ready to put the iPod on the table and start the remembering process.

Jack's initial response, like lots of brave teenagers, was to answer "Whatever."

As his parents told me, he sat and stared at the iPod for the entire hour the first night, continually shaking his head, sighing, and saying, "I just can't remember." He did much the same on the second night. His parents told me by the third night he looked guilty and uncomfortable and unhappy with the situation he found himself in. He seemed caught between a rock and a hard place. On the one hand, he probably wanted to admit what he had done and get it over with. On the other hand, he was not ready to face up to his actions.

On the fourth night, Jack caved in. He said tearfully that he couldn't take sitting and staring at it any longer because it made him feel like a thief and a jerk. He admitted he had taken the iPod while visiting the home of a friend. While his friend was in the bathroom, Jack snuck into his sister's room, stuffed it into his pocket, and shouted through the bathroom door that he had to go home.

As you might imagine, the ensuing process was not pleasant. Jack had to take the iPod back and apologize to the friend, his friend's sister, and his friend's parents. The upside? Such a hard lesson in life will rarely be forgotten.

Trick: The Five-Foot Rule for Stealers

Use It On: A young kid (six to nine, or so) whose conscience is still a work in progress.

When to Employ: Once you become aware that your child has something in his pocket or his mouth that you didn't purchase.

What You'll Need: A tape measure.

You might also want to consider a five-foot rule for a young child who tries to steal something like bubblegum or candy or a pocket-size toy. First, do precisely what your mom or dad would have done to you—have him take it back into the store and tell the cashier or manager what he did, and apologize. Then after that, tell him as much as you would like to trust him, he has given you reason not to. Because of this he will now have to stay within five feet of you at all times when out in public. Tell him that he will have to carry the tape measure with him at all times, because it might be necessary to take a quick measurement to make sure he is staying within his proper boundary. Indicate that after a couple of weeks of successfully going to stores and malls, you'll give him back his space. If you give him back his space and he doesn't steal anymore, great! No more five-foot rule. Also, be sure to tell him that you still love him and that you know he will quickly come back to his senses!

SLACKERS

"Each success only buys an
admission ticket to a more difficult problem."

—*Henry Kissinger, German-born American political scientist and winner of
the Nobel Peace Prize, on the potential penalty of hard work*

irst, are you the parent of a gifted slacker? You know—
the kid with an IQ of about a zillion who simply refuses
to make any attempt to work up to his or her intellectual potential (except when it comes to arguing with you, or
playing video games). Second, do you feel an overwhelming
urge to warn that son or daughter that while some of his or
her peers will be forced to make a choice between, say, the
University of Michigan and Stanford, he or she will have an
equally daunting choice: will it be Wendy's, or will it be Taco
Bell? If your answers are yes, then it's likely you'll need some
tricks that can pierce through the fog of complacency that
hangs over the slacker landscape.

Trick: The "Don't Ask Me to Work Too Hard" Meal

Use It On: Committed slackers twelve and up.

When to Employ: When you wake up in a cold sweat in the middle of the night because you dreamed your slacker was thirty-nine, still living with you, and had just asked you what's for dinner.

What You'll Need: Whatever you can find in your refrigerator. Don't be concerned about taste or visual presentation.

Logic and reason will not put a dent in the mind of a child or teen who has decided he wants to do only enough to get by. If you really want to get his attention, you have to do something more dramatic. Perhaps you should introduce him to the concept of the "Don't Ask Me to Work Too Hard" Meal.

There are several options for slacker meals. One goes like this: Make dinner—chicken, for example, with mashed potatoes, green beans, a salad, and a roll. Then, when everything is cooked, heap all of the food on the plate in one nasty mess—mashed potatoes on top of the chicken, green beans on top of the mashed potatoes, and so on. Another interesting alternative is to tell him you don't have enough clean plates and you didn't feel like washing one, so you're just going to serve his dinner in a cereal bowl.

If you want to, you can skip the whole cooking process and simply grab whatever leftovers you have in your fridge.

It might be something like a leftover hamburger patty, some leftover broccoli, some leftover corn, and the end piece from a stale loaf of bread. You can pop all of this into one big mess on a plate, unheated, or just jam it into a bowl.

Predictably, your child is going to refuse to eat what you've prepared, which is perfectly fine. Tell him that you just don't see what the big deal is. Say that since he only puts minimal effort into what he does, you figured he'd understand perfectly well why you'd want to exert only minimal effort too. The real point is to get his attention in a way that will lead to a productive discussion of why he should put more energy into his own life.

Where should you have this discussion? My best advice is to dump all of the smashed-up food and go out for dinner, just the two of you. Be sure to talk about nothing but his interests and his dreams for his future.

I have found that once a child's real interests are acknowledged and channeled into a career path (even if his interests seem like pie in the sky, like wanting to be a professional video game player), his motivation will be activated. Over dinner you could, for instance, discuss how there are programs in college for video game design and computer animation, but that means doing the work to get into college first. Discuss the idea that there are summer programs and workshops that you would be willing to send him to if he puts forth effort. The trick is to find out what really lights him up, and help him head in that direction.

Trick: Slacker-Sized Meals
(as opposed to Super-Sized)

Use It On: Your slacker, eight to fourteen, who expects dessert.

When to Employ: Preferably after a slacker meal, but can be used at snack time (which you can begin referring to as "slack time") just as effectively.

What You'll Need: Ice cream and ice cream cones.

This is what you do: scoop out a lump of ice cream about the size of a grape and pop it into the bottom of a cone. Hand the cone to your child, and tell him you didn't want to put a lot of effort into making his ice cream cone, but you hope he enjoys it anyway. If he has to peer way down into the cone to see his ice cream, you've hit your target.

Here's the second version of this: instead of dropping his little ball of ice cream into a cone, drop it into a bowl and give him a fork to eat it with. When he complains about the fork, explain that you just grabbed the first thing you could get your hands on in the silverware drawer and he should be grateful you didn't grab the butter knife.

Of course your child is going to be irritated when you hand him the cone with the grape-sized lump of ice cream rattling around at the bottom, or the bowl. He's going to want to get the ice cream out himself and load up his cone or bowl.

This is when you engage him in a talk about the fact that he has not been putting sufficient effort into his life.

One boy I talked to alone about slacker sizing had an interesting perspective. Instead of being defiant or claiming it wouldn't bother him, he promised me that he would change his slacker ways immediately, because he was certain that his mother was exactly the type of mother who would use such a trick. What was interesting, however, was that he actually *asked* me to tell her about it when I brought her into my office later to summarize our session. The *real* reason he wanted me to tell his mother? So she would use it on his sister who, he assured me, was a *real pain in the you know what.*

Trick: The Slacker Computer

Use It On: Slacker nerds.

When to Employ: When your slacker nerd, age twelve to fourteen, does little other than engage in combat with aliens in the virtual world, combat with you in the real world, and otherwise fail to live up to his abilities in any other phase of his life.

What You'll Need: eBay, Craigslist, or a Goodwill store.

Chances are your slacker is like most of his friends in his desire for a top-notch computer. Tell him, however, that the computer you intend to provide will be *equalized* to the level of his efforts unless you see some rapid change. Explain that if you have to go through with this idea, you will get on eBay or Craigslist, where you can get a ten-year-old computer for $19.95. Or, you can go to the Goodwill store where they sometimes sell electronics for as low as $1.39 per pound. Talk about bang for your buck! Tell him it will probably take several days to load one of his games, or a week to download a music video. However, it will work perfectly fine for typing assignments and papers for school.

Tell your slacker that there are several statements you want him to incorporate as personal mantras: Work hard, play hard, but never forget which one comes first. Want the good stuff? Work harder; all things are earned, and nothing is for free.

Do not lose sight of the age-old notion that the best way to get someone to make a positive change is to deliver positive reinforcement. One father ultimately decided to change his son's curfew to an hour later because he agreed to decrease his video game time and voluntarily went to math tutoring. His father's offer of a slacker computer provided him the jump start he needed to get going.

Trick: GPA Poker

Use It On: High school slackers who think they will magically waltz into college regardless of their work habits.

When to Employ: Best to start in the ninth grade.

What You'll Need: Computer access to college websites.

Many slackers will tell you they want to go to college, but most have little insight into today's admission standards. One young man who was beginning his junior year in high school and, according to his mother, was vastly underperforming in relation to his potential, told me he intended to go to Virginia Tech, mainly because he liked their football team. I asked him how his grades were holding up. He said his grades were just fine, something on the order of a 2.5, which shows he's passing everything. I told him the average GPA for the entering freshman class at Tech was much closer to a 4.0 than it was to a 2.5, and said we would have to put together a program of serious grade rehabilitation for him to have any chance of meeting his goal. When he told me that he didn't believe my numbers were accurate, I suggested he simply get on Tech's website and look up the profile for the entering freshman class.

If you have a slacker who wants to go to college but is totally naive about what it will take to get in, you can play GPA poker with him. In GPA poker, you remove the decimal point so that, for example, a 3.50 becomes 350, a 2.87 becomes 287, and so on. Then you sit down with your slacker and both of you guess what number it will take to get into any particular college or university. If either of you are within 15 points, you score a point. If you can get within 15 points for any given school, chances are you have a decent awareness of that institution's admission standards. Make a list of between five and ten colleges and see who ends up with the most points. You'll be surprised at just how much you'll learn about a college by visiting its website.

Your task? Make sure this is a fun exercise, not an exercise in rubbing your slacker's nose in his misperceptions about college. If you decide to play it, order a pizza and get everyone involved. It's good to make sure that all of the children in your family have a realistic view of the grades they'll need in order to get into their chosen school. (It's also likely to show most parents that their own high school grades would no longer get them into the colleges they graduated from years ago, a point that should make them more sympathetic to what their college-bound children are facing today.)

THE COMPLAINT AND
BLAME DEPARTMENT

"Man invented language to satisfy his deep need to complain."
—*Lily Tomlin, American actress and comedian*

Y ou have to be careful about how you interpret your child's complaining. For some children, a constantly dour, negative viewpoint is a big red flag that they're depressed. As I said earlier in the book, you never use tricks on a depressed child. Get him or her into counseling instead.

However, some kids complain because it's just too difficult to make them happy unless the world is catering to their every need and whim. In addition, they might be modeling the same behaviors that they see their parents doing at home. Parents, time to go take a peek in the mirror. Are you doing too much complaining or negative talk? If so, you can hardly blame your child for doing the same.

Trick: Pre-Complaining

Use It On: Kids six to twelve who tend to wreck the fun with their constant complaints.

When to Employ: Before you leave to go do something fun.

What You'll Need: Tickets or passes to an amusement park would make for a great opportunity. A trip to a museum will work.

Is your child the one who always manages to find something to carp about when everyone else is having the time of their lives? "I'm hot. I'm cold. I don't feel good. This place stinks. This is booooooring." And so on. If so, you might want to tell her prior to your next fun event or outing that you are considering having her *pre-complain*. When she asks what you are talking about, explain that she has developed the bad habit of complaining, which tends to wreck everyone else's fun. So in order to bring a halt to this process, you are considering having her go into a room alone for a few minutes before you leave, or before the fun event begins, so she can complain out loud for several minutes to drain it all out of her system. You can act it out for her: "I don't like this. You said this was going to be fun and it isn't. I want to stop doing this and do something really fun. I don't know why you made me come here. You lied to me about this place. Why do we have to stay? Nobody thinks this place is fun." And so on.

Ask your child if she thinks it might be useful to have her do this prior to, for example, going to the beach. If she says no, ask her to make a solemn promise that she will not complain once you get there. Be sure to point out, however, that if she does start to complain at the beach, all is not lost. You will let her walk fifty yards down the beach to a private spot, and she can stand or sit there in the sand and complain for five minutes straight. Once she has stopped, she can come rejoin the group. Tell her that she could do a similar sort of "draining the complaining" at an amusement park, a pool party, at the movies, wherever complaining might occur.

The truth of this trick? I have told it to many, many complainers but have never heard of anyone actually having to use it. The mere mention of it at the start of a complaining jag ("Sweetheart, do you need to go off somewhere alone so you can drain your complaining?") seems to shut the complaining down immediately.

Trick: The Blame Game

Use It On: Kids six to twelve who blame you, or others, for everything they do wrong.

When to Employ: When you're up to your eyeballs with their excuses.

What You'll Need: A box of pancake mix.

If you have a child who constantly denies that her mistakes are her own fault, and in particular if she constantly puts the blame off on you, consider doing *this* next Saturday: once she's up, begin making a potentially delicious breakfast while at the same time making small talk with her. Pancakes, let's say. Intentionally cook the pancakes until they are hard and rubbery and serve them to her. When she complains, tell her it's all *her* fault because she was talking to you and she made you forget all about the pancakes. This is what it might sound like:

Child: "These pancakes are horrible! What did you do to them?"

You: "*Me*?! This is all *your* fault. I didn't do anything wrong!"

Child: "What? It's not *my* fault. You're the one who overcooked them!"

You: "You *made* me mess up. It is too your fault!"

Child: "No, it's not! I didn't do anything to you!"

You: "Yes, you did! You were talking too much. I couldn't concentrate or focus on anything!"

Child: "What?"

You: "Not *my* fault!"

Make sure this exercise leads to a calm discussion of how you want her to do less blaming and become more accepting of her own mistakes. You might want to teach her to use a self-statement that I used with my own kids and hundreds of others at my office: "Mistakes are no big deal. You just acknowledge them, fix them, and move on."

Trick: Kid Cooks

Use It On: Children six to twelve who routinely complain about the food you make.

When to Employ: The next time they say, "What? Homemade lasagna again?" Or something along those lines.

What You'll Need: Dinner items in the fridge.

This one is just pure old-fashioned common sense. When your kids complain too often about what you make for dinner, say, "I've got a great idea!" Compliment them on how creative they are, then tell them they are to cook and serve dinner the following night and clean up as well, since this is what you always do. If they ask you what they're supposed to cook, tell them to go see what's in the fridge or cupboard and figure it out on their own.

Better yet, inform your children that they are now going to be tasked with cooking meals once per week. It would be a good idea to get a special cookbook for children, with recipes your kids can handle. Who knows—in your effort to give them a taste of their own medicine, you may uncover a budding chef who will actually want to come up with something delicious. Nothing wrong with dreaming, right? And by the way, if you do this, your children may learn to cooperate with each other, at least for a couple of hours once per week. At the very least, they'll learn how to feed themselves.

SCHOOL DAYS,
SCHOOL DAZE

"All people have the right to stupidity,
but some abuse the privilege."
—*Anonymous*

Back in the good old days, if a child was forgetful and dreamy, everyone chuckled, referred to him as an "absentminded professor," and worked at helping the child learn to overcome his absentminded ways. If you forgot to hand in your homework, your teacher didn't worry that it might hurt your feelings or destroy your self-concept when she put your name on the board. You just had to deal with it and do better because, if you didn't, she'd do the same thing again the next day. If you rushed through your work and handed in something so sloppy that your teacher couldn't read it, or your final product was only partially completed, it was easy to guess what you'd spend recess doing.

Those days are gone. Today, we send our absentminded professors to doctors to get diagnosed and medicated. But that's another story entirely. In many cases these children can learn to be more attentive and motivated. Here are some tricks . . .

Trick: The "I Forgot" Pizza Method

Use It On: Kids eight to fourteen who can't seem to remember to do their homework or to hand it in if and when they do it.

When to Employ: After your child's next school notice about missing homework.

What You'll Need: A friend at your local pizza parlor.

There is currently an epidemic of children not turning in homework. To be more precise, there is an epidemic of *boys* not turning in homework. (Girls, for the most part, seem to know better.) What's the cause of this? As strange as it might sound, in some schools it's simply not cool to be thought of as smart. In yet other schools it just seems to be something in the air, or perhaps the water—none of the males take homework seriously. Lots of times, to be blunt, boys are spending so much time doing combat in the virtual world that they no longer have time for such mundane issues as English assignments.

The problem with this, of course, is all the missing homework absolutely shreds grades by the end of a marking period. I looked at a printout the teacher of a seventh grader sent me for the marking period. He had six tests/quizzes, and his grades were four 100s, a 90 and an 80, which averaged out to 95. However, on his fifteen or so homework assignments he had one 60, and the rest zeros because he failed to turn anything in. The end result was that his average for the marking period was a 55, despite his successes on tests!

If this is going on at your house, you might want to consider the fact that pizza is one of your most potent weapons. Let me tell you about the "I forgot" pizza solution.

Call your favorite pizza place. When you make your order, do your best to assure the person on the other end of the phone line that you are not making a prank phone call. Their mistrust will be due to the fact that you want a pizza on which there is no cheese, with only a bit of sauce rubbed randomly around the edges of the crust, and a few scattered pieces of pepperoni.

When you bring it home, be prepared for your kids to be outraged. Your job is to point out that whoever made the pizza must have "forgotten" to put on all the ingredients, much like your kids "forget" to do their homework, or "forget" to turn it in. Then say, "Oh well," point out that there's plenty of sandwich material in the fridge, and walk away.

By the way, if you really want to intensify the pizza trick, just bring home an empty pizza box. When your kids open it and demand to know what the deal is, tell them that the kid at the pizza place must have decided to just skip this assignment completely, just like they do with their homework.

Trick: The Lost Pizza Method

Use It On: Kids six to fourteen who actually do their homework but manage to lose it before they can turn it in.

When to Employ: After the incomplete-homework notices begin to pile up.

What You'll Need: A frozen pizza, a jar of peanut butter, a movie your child will love, and some Barney DVDs.

Here's another pizza trick, this time for use with the type of child who does his homework, then promptly loses it. One boy I knew was an extreme example of this. He definitely wanted to do well in school. However, after he completed his homework he would either jam it into one of the multiple pockets of his backpack, or slide it into one of the books in his backpack and later forget which book he put it in. Sometimes he would take his homework out to check something, and the bus driver would later find it stuffed down in the seat, or dirty and semi-ripped-up on the floor because everyone had stepped on it as they were exiting the bus. His mother told me when she finally checked the bottom of his school locker, she found eighteen missing assignments. The end result of all this was that his homework rarely made it to his teacher's desk, and his grades were all the worse for it.

If you have a son like this, here's the procedure: inform him on a Friday afternoon when he gets home that since it's the end of the week, it's time to celebrate. Say you're going to bake a pizza, and he can eat it while watching the movie you rented. Tell him to go enjoy himself while the pizza is cooking.

Somewhere along the line he's going to pop into the kitchen and ask if the pizza is ready. It is at this point that you get a worried look on your face and start to look all around the kitchen. Tell him you know you baked the pizza, but you can't find it. Look through the cupboards and drawers and even the garbage pail. Finally, say to him, "I swear I baked that pizza. You've got to believe me. But I can't find it. I guess I'll just have to make you a peanut butter sandwich. Sorry."

He'll probably ask you where you put the movie you rented, his thinking being that at least he can eat his sandwich while he watches the movie. Get that worried look on your face again and start looking through the drawers and cabinets, including the trash. Then say, "Oh my gosh—I can't find the movie either! I know I stopped and got it, but I can't find it now. I must have misplaced it. Oh well, all is not lost. We have your old Barney DVDs that you can watch while you eat your sandwich."

After the shock of not getting the pizza and movie has registered, he's probably going to realize you've played a trick on him. At this point, tell him the two of you need to talk about the impact of his forgetfulness on his grades and achievement, and you need to discuss a new strategy to help him keep track of his homework. Tell him that after you've discussed a very simple strategy, such as having a separate folder only for the homework assignments he has to turn in, you will take out the pizza you have hidden in the refrigerator and you'll take out the movie you also hid. Warn him, however, that you have many more tricks up your sleeve if he does not put more effort into keeping his work organized.

Be sure to reward him for his efforts to improve. If you are of the mind-set that children should not be rewarded for doing what they should be doing in the first place, be careful. If it was easy for your child to master these skills, he would have mastered them already. Using positive reinforcement gives you the opportunity to help him master them more quickly.

Trick: Rushing Through Homework

Use It On: Kids eight to twelve who rush through their homework so they can get to the truly important stuff, like *texting*.

When to Employ: When your child is capable of A/B work, but gets C/D grades due to rushing through.

What You'll Need: A great movie, and two bags of unpopped popcorn. Your child is likely to supply you with all the bad grades you need to pull this one off.

Here's yet another food-based strategy, for as we know kids will do just about anything for their favorite treat or snack. This one is for the child who rushes through her homework, doing only a minimal job so she can quickly get to her bedroom and start texting her BFF (best friend forever). Try this instead of grounding her or taking away her cell phone: explain to her on a Friday after school that you have rented a movie she really wants to see, and you're going to pop some popcorn to go with it. However, explain that you intend to see if the popcorn that should be microwaved for three minutes will be ready in one minute because you want to get the cooking over with as quickly as possible. Be prepared for one of those "Are you clueless?" looks.

Also, tell her you hope she doesn't mind, but you want to fast-forward through the boring parts of the movie, stopping only at the good parts. She's bound to protest, but go ahead with your plan. Undercook the popcorn and put it in a nice big bowl. Put in the DVD and move through it in spurts, acting all the while as if there's nothing wrong with missing most of the scenes. Let her live with this situation for ten minutes or so and then stop, heave a sigh of relief, and ask her if she has gotten the point.

When she looks at you with total puzzlement, tell her that you haven't gone loco, and in a few minutes you intend to put in a new bag of popcorn and cook it properly, and to go back to the start of the movie and watch it at regular speed. But tell her you'll do this only after the two of you have come to an agreement that she will stop rushing through her homework. If she does not, the quality of her education will be roughly equal to the quality of the movie and popcorn event she just went through.

Also, you and she must come to an agreement about how much time will be devoted to studying and homework on a daily basis before phones of any sort can be used. Make a rule that you will keep her cell phone while she's doing homework, because the beeping or flashing that signals a new text message will interrupt her over and over and one day she'll end up with an attention span that's about two minutes long.

Also remind her that if she refuses to follow a reasonable set of guidelines about phone calls and texting, you will simply have to take her cell phone away and keep it until her grades recover. Promise her that you will truly go through with this (but only if you really will). As with all tricks, follow-through is key if you don't see change. And remember, you can use this technique with children eight to twelve, who are rushing through homework, even when their rushing has nothing to do with phones or texting. You can use it with kids who rush through so they can go play video games, go shoot hoops, go surf the Web, go play with Barbies, and so on. Feel free to be inventive.

After this discussion (which by the way should be short and sweet and not some droning, mind-numbing lecture), sit back for popcorn and a movie.

I DON'T
KNOW

"We don't do 'I don't know' around me."
—*Dr. Riley's immediate response when children
attempt to use the three-word disclaimer in his office*

The children I work with find out rapidly that one thing
I will not accept is answering "I don't know" to questions. I wheedle and nag and tease them into answering
by reminding them that my office is a place where people
come to think. I also remind kids that it is doubtful any major
problem was ever solved by uttering those three bad words.
If you have a child who has begun to automatically answer
you by saying "I don't know," or answers you by giving such
vague responses that no real information has actually been
transmitted, give the tricks in this section a try.

Trick: "My Brain Does Not Work"

Use It On: Kids eight to twelve who answer any and all questions by saying "I don't know."

When to Employ: When they persist, even though you've explained that "I don't know" is not an acceptable answer at your house.

What You'll Need: A list of things they won't be allowed to do if their brains don't work. A wingback chair will also be helpful.

Lots of children, big and little, develop the "I don't know" reflex. You ask a question, they immediately respond "I don't know." The problem, of course, is that when kids do this they never actually learn to think. If you have an I-don't-know child at your house, you probably should sit down with him and ask, "What is your brain's job?" Your child will likely answer like this:

"I don't know."

"Then let me tell you. Your brain's job is to know stuff. If your brain does not know stuff, it cannot protect you and keep you alive."

"Whatever."

"Well, here's the problem. If your brain doesn't work, we cannot allow you to use complex electro-mechanical devices because of the danger they pose."

"Huh?"

"Things like a PlayStation or an Xbox or a Wii. If your brain doesn't work, you might mess them up."

"Yeah, right!"

"It's true. And we can't let you ride a bike, either. You might run yourself into a tree if your brain doesn't work. And you can't use any handheld video game because you might try to flush it down the toilet or make a sandwich out of it, or who knows what."

"This is so lame!"

Reiterate that if your child's brain continues not to function, it may be best for him to ignore his fantasies of driving automobiles, or even going outside alone without supervision. You might even point out that if his brain doesn't work, the only safe thing you can allow him to do is sit in a nice, big, protective wingback chair because there is very little chance of him falling out and hurting himself.

Tell him the way to get you to back off should be obvious. The "I don't knows" have gotta go, or any devices with electrons or gears will have to disappear.

> ## Trick: The Mandatory "I Don't Know"
>
> **Use It On:** Children eight to fourteen who absolutely *insist* on answering every question with "I don't know."
>
> **When to Employ:** Know how they say we only use 10 percent of our brain? Use this trick when it is evident that your child is down to about half of that.
>
> **What You'll Need:** Bologna and some stale bread might come in handy.

If you have children or teens who simply refuse to modify their use of the three-word disclaimer, you might want to try a trick based on the draining procedures we've used earlier with kids who say bad words, or who make obnoxious noises. The Mandatory "I Don't Know" requires you to sit down and explain to your child that for some mysterious reason, there are so many "I don't knows" in his system that you've decided to drain them all out this Saturday. The only way the "I don't knows" can be drained out is for him to answer "I don't know" to every question you ask:

"Sam, what would you like for lunch?"

"I don't know, Mom."

"I could go to Subway and get you a sub. Would you like that?"

"I told you, Mom, I don't know."

"What a shame. I would have thought you'd enjoy doing that. Oh well, I guess since you don't know what you'd like for lunch, I'll just make you a bologna sandwich. Would you like some chips or a soda with it?"

"I don't know, Mom."

"OK, just plain bologna on bread, then."

If nothing else, this trick will leave your child much more attuned to the fact that those three little words have become a reflex.

Trick: The Nano Information Specialist

Use It On: Eight- to fourteen-year-olds who persist on giving you vague answers.

When to Employ: When you've had it with getting no information whatsoever every time you try to talk with your child.

What You'll Need: A willingness to be exceptionally vague. This will be easy for most dads, not so for most moms.

You may have heard or read about nano machines. These are devices made to be as small as absolutely possible, which is sort of like the amount of information some kids try to give you when you ask them a question. For example:

"Who are you going out with tonight?"

"Friends."

Answers like this make you nuts because they either give you no information or they give you so little information that you end up feeling like you know less than you did before you asked the question. Kids and teens who have adopted this as an answering style, however, believe they have given you a legitimate answer, and they wonder what the problem is when you get all excited over their vagueness.

Sometimes it helps to give these types a taste of their own vagueness. I'll do this at my office sometimes when I'm getting nano information out of a kid. For example, I'll say,

"I will give you a dollar if you can guess what kind of vehicle I drive. You can ask me up to ten questions about it, and after you feel like you've got enough information, you get to take one guess. I'll even help you with the questions. You can ask things like how many doors it has, if it sits up high or sits low to the ground, what color it is, where it was made, how big a motor it has, and so on. Give it a try."

"This is lame."

"I know. But it's designed to show you what it feels like trying to talk to you. Go ahead, give it a try."

"OK. How many doors does it have?"

"I only use one at a time."

"Does it sit up high or does it sit down low?"

"That depends on how tall you are."

"What color is it?"

"Paint color."

"What kind of tires does it have?"

"Round ones."

"Where was it made?"

"In a car factory."

"I give up. Keep your money."

Here's another variation of the Nano Information Specialist trick. In this one, *any* question your child asks you gets nano information.

Child: "What's for dinner?"

Parent: "Food."

Child: "OK, Mom. What kind of food?"

Parent: "The kind of food you eat."

Child: "What kind of food that you eat?"

Parent: "The kind that you put in your mouth and chew."

Child: "What kind that you put in your mouth and chew?"

Parent: "The kind that you chew and swallow."

And so on . . .

The point here is to teach your child through direct experience just how frustrating it is to be on the receiving end of nano answers.

WET TOWELS, TOOTHPASTE TUBES, AND OTHER BATHROOM BATTLES

Even when freshly washed and relieved of all obvious confections, children tend to be sticky.

—*Fran Lebowitz, American author*

Have you noticed that the smallest room in the house can become the one where the biggest battles take place? One kid hogs the bathroom doing who knows what while another bangs on the door doing the peepee dance and screaming that he's got to go *right now*! Or one kid uses up all the hot water in the morning, leaving the rest of you to take cold showers. And then there's the kid who simply *will not* go in to take her bath unless you physically pick her up and put her there.

It all makes you wonder if your kids have developed some sort of neurosis about the bathroom: do they get pleasure out of causing bladder pain for their siblings; are they working out their oppositional drives by making you tell them over and over that it's time to stop playing and get in the tub? In any case, if bathroom battles have robbed your home of peace, quiet, and cooperation, you may find some of the following tricks to be useful.

Trick: Bath Time Now

Use It On: Kids who take *forever* to get into the tub.

When to Employ: When bedtime routinely gets delayed because Mister or Miss Pokey won't stop what he or she is doing and get in the tub.

What You'll Need: All you need is some bubble bath and a functioning bathtub. Can't do this one with a shower.

This is for the child who refuses to get in the tub when you ask her to. Go run a tub of water, and tell her this is her bathwater for the night. Point out that it is pleasantly warm and soapy right now, but soon the bubbles will be gone and the water will be cooled off and things will not be nearly so comfy or fun to bathe in.

If she takes too long to get into the tub, she may have a surprise waiting! In truth, the water will not get any cooler than room temperature. While it may not be comfortable to sit in, she can always stand in the water and bathe herself quickly. It is unlikely she will want to do this more than once. Tell her you will run the water for her again tomorrow night and if she makes a good decision, she'll get to enjoy a nice warm soak.

Trick: The Après Shower Program

Use It On: Tweeners and teens who can't manage to hang up their wet towels.

When to Employ: When you don't want the finish on your furniture or floor to get wrecked.

What You'll Need: Paper towels, extra absorbent.

Lots of tweens and teens get out of the tub or shower and head to the bedroom to towel off. Too often they drape their wet towels over the footboard of their bed, a chair, or the dresser, or they simply drop the towel in a wet lump onto your hardwood floor. The problem with this, other than looking sloppy, is that over time it destroys the finish on the furniture or the floor.

There's a simple fix. Tell your child if she does not break this habit by a certain date (give her about a week to improve), you will buy a roll of paper towels she can use for drying herself after her bath. Say you will even pop for the extra-absorbent ones. As always, remind her if she solves this bad habit rapidly, you will get off her back—the yelling and screaming and arguing over this issue will almost *magically* go away—and she will be able to continue to enjoy the big, comfy bath towels you provide.

Trick: Grounded from the Tube

Use It On: Kids who can't manage to screw the top back on the toothpaste tube.

When to Employ: When there is so much goop all over the toothpaste tube that you can't even screw the top back on.

What You'll Need: A new tube of toothpaste.

If your children have developed the habit of leaving the top off the toothpaste tube, to the point that when you try to use it you get goop all over your hand, tell them you're considering putting them on a toothpaste tube program. This will entail buying a new tube and putting it in the bathroom. As long as they remember to put the top back on and not leave it in a mess, everything will be hunky-dory. However, if they begin to leave the top off again and the tube becomes messy, they will officially be grounded from using the toothpaste tube. Instead, you will put a bowl on the bathroom sink, and squirt a week's worth of toothpaste into it for them to use. You will put plastic wrap over the bowl so the toothpaste will remain moist. Be sure to point out that there is little you can do if they fail to wrap the bowl back up after they use it. In that case, they may have to add a little water and mix it all up to make it useable again.

If your children complain loudly about this, tell them there is a convenient alternative: you will supervise them in practice sessions of screwing the cap back onto the tube. Explain that it is obvious from a rigorous scientific viewpoint that they have absolutely no trouble at all getting the top off. Getting it back on, however, appears to be a mysterious impossibility.

Trick: Bathroom Monopolizer

Use It On: Children eight to fourteen who won't get out of the bathroom, even though others are screaming that they need to use it too.

When to Employ: Once it's clear that the monopolizer thinks the bathroom is his or her exclusive turf.

What You'll Need: A calendar.

Here's a trick to use with the child who seems to believe that the bathroom belongs to her. Explain that the cleaning of the bathroom will now be proportional to the amount of time *spent* in the bathroom. It only makes sense, right? Tell your monopolizer that because she spends so much time in the bathroom, she will be responsible for cleaning it three Saturdays a month, while the rest of the family will be responsible for the fourth cleaning. Mark out the dates on the calendar to avoid confusion over which weekend belongs to whom. And don't forget to point out that on those odd months that have five weekends, guess who gets to do the extra? In 2011, for example, the year this book was published, those months were January, April, July, October, and December. Most likely just describing this plan will make your monopolizer think twice about acting like the queen of the bathroom.

Trick: Hot-Water Hogs

Use It On: Children eight to fourteen who routinely use up all the hot water, leaving everyone else to experience the exhilaration of a cold morning shower.

When to Employ: The next time you get ice cubes when you were hoping for steam.

What You'll Need: You need a pair of pliers and a house. Might not be able to use this one if you live in an apartment building.

This one is simple for people who have access to their hot water heater. Once your hot-water hog is in the shower, turn off the hot water. Don't be surprised if he or she comes screaming at you wrapped in a towel, angry as a wet cat. Your explanation: "Just wanted to show you what it's like."

Alternatively, if your child doesn't necessarily use up all the hot water, but just stays and stays and stays in the shower, resulting in a huge water bill, simply turn off the water at its source after an acceptable time.

SIBLING COMBAT

"Brothers and sisters are as close as hands and feet."
—Vietnamese proverb

I f you have more than one child, you know all about sibling combat. Children placed in close proximity are bound to find something to fight about. Lots of times they're bored and stir things up to be entertained. Often, one child feels like the other is favored by the parents. Sometimes their personalities are simply like oil and water—they don't mix well, and it may take them until well after puberty to learn to be around each other civilly. In any case, if you have gone the traditional route of warnings, time-outs, and family meetings, and *still* your kids battle night and day, you should introduce them to the tricks that follow.

Trick: The Failure to Spend Enough Time Together Program

Use It On: Kids six to fourteen who are in constant combat with each other.

When to Employ: Basically, after you've had enough of their hitting, kicking, shoving, whacking, tattling, and volume.

What You'll Need: One room with a door that works, some books, some paper, and some pencils.

I once knew a mom who had a son and a daughter (eleven and eight, respectively) who fought like the proverbial cat and dog. Evenings and weekends were wrecked with their squabbling. Literally *anything* could set off a major fight, such as the sound of the other one eating or breathing. They would even complain about the way the other one smelled.

Here's the trick we used: I sat down with the children and explained, quite seriously, that the reason they fought so much was that they had failed to spend enough time together. I told them it was now their mom's job to make sure they spent much, much more time together. In order to accomplish this, on the coming Saturday their mom would get them up at 7 in the morning so they could get cleaned up and have breakfast. At 8 they would go into a room together, the door would be closed, and they would not be allowed to come out until noon. Their mom had a perfect spot for this, an essentially empty guest room. It had a bed and a dresser and that was it. I told them they would be allowed to take a couple of books, paper, and a pencil into the room in case they wanted to spend their time reading, writing, or drawing. Nothing else would be allowed. No video games, no toys, no music, no Legos, no Barbies, no nothing but books, paper, and pencil.

Then I explained the ground rules. As long as they got along well and did not yell, scream, argue, or fight, their time together would be over at noon and they could come out. However, if they got into a fight, their mom would break it up and send each of them to their rooms for a thirty-minute time-out, during which they were allowed to do nothing other than think about their own behavior. After the thirty minutes, they would go back into the guest room. An additional thirty minutes would then be added to the amount of time they had to stay in the guest room together, which would mean their exit time would now be 12:30, not 12:00. I also explained if they continued to fight and their mother had to intervene again, they would get another super-boring thirty-minute time-out, after which they would go back into the room together, with their exit time now being 1:00. It could go on and on like this for the entire day if they continued to squabble. In their particular case, the mother had to intervene twice, adding two extra time-outs before it dawned on the kids she was not bluffing.

This trick had quite an impact on their squabbling. All their mother had to do afterward, when they were gearing up for a fight, was ask them if they had spent enough time together recently. Most kids, when they hear me tell this story, laugh out loud. At the same time, they also pledge to change their arguing and squabbling ways. Hearing about this technique is sort of like watching someone slip on a banana peel: it makes you want to laugh, even though you know it's impolite. But you certainly don't want it happening to you.

Trick: Grounded from Your Mouth
Times Two (or More)

Use It On: Kids six to fourteen who argue with each other too much (or who argue with you too much).

When to Employ: When you'd rather staple your ears shut than have to listen to one more fight.

What You'll Need: All you need are two or more kids. They will naturally provide the arguing.

In Chapter 1, I talked about grounding a child from his mouth if he argues too much. However, you can also use a version of this if you have two (or more) children who argue incessantly with each other, particularly if you do not have an entire day to devote to having your children experience quality time together in the guest room. Here's a simple solution: announce to your kids that they are now officially grounded from their mouths for one full hour.

This is bound to get a resounding "Huh?" out of them. Your explanation is that for the next hour they are not to use their mouths. That means no words or sounds are to come out of their mouths, and no drinks or snacks are to go into their mouths. Any meals falling into that time frame will have to be delayed.

Also, be sure to warn them that if either of them is unable to stay quiet and breaks the silence, they will start the hour all over again. And if they continue to argue after you've used this trick, tell them it obviously did not work because they were not grounded from their mouths long enough. The next time will be for an hour and a half.

Remember, there are very few siblings who do not argue. Don't worry, they'll grow out of it sooner or later. Use this trick to ensure that it is indeed sooner rather than later.

Trick: Car Time-Out

Use It On: Sibs, age six to twelve, who are at war in the back-seat.

When to Employ: When you have warned them twice to tamp down the fighting, but they have not.

What *They'll* Need: Two hands. You won't need a thing.

What if the fighting takes place in the car, far, far away from home and the bedrooms typically used for time-out? You can do Car Time-Out! How is this done? Simple enough: your children have to put one hand over their mouths, and one hand over their eyes. Have them sit this way for five minutes, which should be enough time for them to think about their behavior. And, oh, one ground rule: if you catch them peeking, they have to start all over. If after five minutes they keep the peace, no more Car Time-Out. However, you can always give them another five-minute round if they start to fight again.

One mom I know has come to use Car Time-Out routinely on her local drives, not just on long trips. She has two boys who struggle with each other over any conceivable issue once they're in the backseat of her car: "He's got his hand on my half of the seat! He's looking out my window, make him look out his own window! He's breathing on me!" And so on.

She had tried every method under the sun to get them to stop, because their arguing could turn even a drive to their favorite ice cream place into a miserable experience. Now all she has to do is say "Would a few minutes of Car Time-Out help you guys settle the argument?" Invariably, they bring it to a halt.

Trick: The 7-Eleven Solution

Use It On: Kids six to fourteen who are screaming at each other in the car.

When to Employ: In the summer, when the screaming gets so bad that you want to jump out of the car.

What You'll Need: A 7-Eleven store.

Let's say it's a nice, warm summer day, you have to drive somewhere, and your kids are screaming and yelling and ignoring everything you've said in an attempt to bring the fighting to a halt. Try this instead: pull into a 7-Eleven convenience store. When your kids ask what you're going to get in the store, say nothing.

Go in and buy yourself one of those Slurpee frozen drinks that 7-Eleven stores are so famous for, or maybe a candy bar or a Popsicle. Once you've made your purchase, go back to your car and lean against the front fender, where the kids can see you sipping your drink, or eating your treat. Explain that you needed a break from their fighting, and this is the way you chose to get it.

Once they're calm, get back into your car and continue your drive. If it's a long drive, tell them if you're happy with their behavior in an hour or two, you'll make another stop. Maybe you'll buy them something too.

Trick: The Ten-Foot Rule for Multiple Users

Use It On: Two or more kids who can't be close to each other without fighting.

When to Employ: Once it is scientifically proven that this equation holds in your family: P = C (proximity equals conflict).

What You'll Need: A measuring tape.

This one is simple enough. If your kids are fighting too much, tell them you are considering using the Ten-Foot Rule. In this procedure, they are no longer allowed to be within ten feet of each other. Get your tape measure out and have them measure what this distance will actually look like. Warn them that while they probably won't think this is any big deal, they need to get their eyes wide open. They'll be eating in shifts unless you have a table that is more than ten feet long. Obviously it makes going anywhere in the car together virtually impossible. So, they should just plan on going nowhere until the conflict stops.

If you try the Ten-Foot Rule and your kids discover long-distance fighting, don't lose hope! Remind them you always have the option of instituting the "no longer allowed in the same room" rule. Or, if you need to intensify this further and you have a house with at least two levels, warn your children one of them can rapidly become the upstairs kid, and one of them can become the downstairs kid.

You may be surprised how telling your children that they *must* stay apart from each other will have the almost magical, paradoxical effect of making them *want* to be together and get along, almost as if to show you that your stupid trick won't work. It's weird!

Trick: The Ten-Foot Rule
for Regaining the Peace

Use It On: The kid in your family, six to twelve, who always stirs the pot.

When to Employ: When you need more control over your little instigator.

What You'll Need: That measuring tape we talked about earlier.

There's yet another variation of the Ten-Foot Rule that you can use if you have a child who just can't seem to tolerate peace. We're talking about the child who is always badgering his brothers and sisters, or trying to get them to do his dirty work for him.

Garrett was a boy I worked with who kept the whole family on edge because he liked to scare everyone when they least expected it, to trip his sister, or to reach in and turn out the lights when his brother was in the bathroom.

Tell your instigator that if he has difficulty keeping the peace with his sibs, like Garrett, you will be forced to keep him within ten feet of you at all times in order to observe his behavior. Give him a clear explanation of what his life will be like: if you decide, for example, to go sit and watch some stupid show on TV, he will have to be in the same room with you, no more than ten feet away. If you get up to go to the kitchen to cook dinner or clean up, he will have to go with you. If you decide to take a shower, he will have to sit outside the bathroom door until you are done. And so on.

Several hours of this, tops, will surely bore him silly and will have him begging for a chance to show you he'll be good. You'll want to remind him that he always has the choice to knock it off with bothering everyone, which means you won't have to use this trick ever again.

Trick: Child in Charge

Use It On: Kids ten and up who like to rule the roost.

When to Employ: Once the older child has her role in the family confused with the parent's role.

What You'll Need: A younger sibling who seems to be life's major source of irritation for that older sibling.

While it's natural for children to want to exercise more power and influence within their family system, some children take it too far. Sonya was twelve and was all over her six-year-old sister, Maddy. She complained about anything and everything Maddy did, and constantly tried to boss and micromanage her.

I asked Sonya if she really would like to be Maddy's boss. She nodded enthusiastically and said that she couldn't wait to do lots and lots of punishments. I burst that particular bubble. I explained that being in charge would actually mean taking care of her sister. She would have to get up early Saturday morning to make breakfast. After that, she'd have to find something to occupy Maddy for the morning, such as games or crafts or other activities. Maybe she could get on the phone and arrange for some of Maddy's little friends to come over. While they were playing would be a good opportunity to change the sheets and do Maddy's laundry. That night, after she made dinner, she'd have to make sure Maddy took her bath. And there was no way Maddy could go to sleep without being read her bedtime story.

The term "wholesale retreat" is what best describes her reaction to learning what being in charge would really be like. She instantly decided she had better things to do.

Trick: Pet Empathy

Use It On: Kids six to twelve who constantly argue and fight with each other about whose turn it is to feed the pets.

When to Employ: When it occurs to you that being your kid's hamster must feel like being trapped in the seventh ring of hell.

What You'll Need: The type of pet that needs to be fed at least once a day.

Do your children argue with each other over who's going to feed their pets? Do you have a spouse or a significant other? If so, try this: get into a "discussion" in front of your kids over whose turn it is to make dinner. (Be careful not to get too intense with this. The purpose is to open your children's eyes a bit, not to frighten them.)

You: "I'm not feeding them tonight. I fed them last night! It's your turn!"

Spouse: "But I made lunch for them today. I feed them all the time."

You: "No, you don't. You're imagining that."

Spouse: "I can't believe this! You hardly ever feed them. I feed them constantly."

You: "Well, I'm not feeding them tonight! I'm too tired."

Spouse: "I'm not feeding them tonight either, because I'm just as tired as you!"

You: "But they're hungry!"

Spouse: "Well?"

You: "Well *what*?"

Let enough time pass for your kids to start to get a bit hungry before you actually make them something to eat. It won't hurt them at all, and it can prompt a good dinnertime discussion: tell your kids they don't eat until their pets have eaten, and stick to it!

Trick: In Service to the Greater Good

Use It On: Kids eight to fourteen who consistently wreck dinner with their arguing.

When to Employ: When your dreams of quality family time around the dinner table have been reduced to nightmares.

What You'll Need: Dinner.

I once worked with a very loving, tolerant set of parents who were being driven nuts by their kids' arguing. These children were absolutely *devoted* to turning the dinner hour into an exercise in conflict. "He's eating all the potatoes!" "She's kicking my chair!" "Stop looking at me!" "*You* stop breathing on *me!*"

I met with the family and told them I was going to use a simple trick to see if it would help make dinner more pleasant. I said that every night, like waiters, the children would have to serve dinner to each other. For example, the oldest could serve dinner to the youngest, who in turn would have to serve the middle child, who in turn would have to serve the oldest. They would have to rotate the pattern nightly, so that they would not be serving the same person each night.

At first, the kids got a manic grin on their faces that told me they were absolutely feasting on the fantasy of just how horrible and sloppy they could make their sibling's plate look.

Then it went in the other direction as it became evident that their sibling might do an equally bad job on *their* plate. "But Joey's too little to know how to serve a plate," the sister said.

"That's OK," I said. "He'll learn."

"But he's gonna make all my food touch each other," she said. "I don't like it when my food touches!"

"Well, if you do right by Joey, I'm sure he will do right by you," I assured her.

As simple as this seems, it had a positive effect. None of them wanted to serve their sibling, or be served, and they all agreed it was better to stop arguing during dinner than have their parents go through with this trick.

Trick: Resume the Role

Use It On: Older kids, those in the ten to fourteen range, who are always complaining that their younger siblings get preferential treatment in the family.

When to Employ: When you absolutely can't get it through your child's head that younger kids and older kids can't be treated exactly the same.

What You'll Need: Two kids in conflict. One older, one younger. If you have at least two kids who weren't born on the same day, you're bound to need this trick sooner or later.

Do you have a child who seems to believe that coming home with a Barney DVD for the younger one and nothing for him constitutes prima facie evidence that he is being neglected? Does he constantly complain that nothing at your house is fair? If so, you might want to have him Resume the Role for one week.

For example, tell your thirteen-year-old that the only way to make things precisely fair is to treat him exactly the same as you treat your eight-year-old. Explain why it will have to be like this: it's not possible to treat an eight-year-old like a thirteen-year-old—he or she hasn't had the proper life experiences. However, the thirteen-year-old has already spent 365 days being eight, and it should be easy enough for him to remember how to do it again.

Point out to the older child that he now has two options. He can be treated precisely like the eight-year-old as regards freedoms, privileges, bedtime, and so on. Or he can knock it off with the complaining.

Trick: A Touch of Class

Use It On: Kids who throw food at each other during dinner.

When to Employ: After one of them falls out of his chair trying to duck a flying dinner roll, and manages to take his plate and glass of milk down with him.

What You'll Need: A Frank Sinatra CD.

Remember how everyone on the old TV shows would get relatively dressed up for dinner? Turns out it's not a bad idea. If you want to teach your children some table manners, once a month have everyone dress up for a wonderful meal (either prepared by you or brought in). Break out the good china and crystal. Your children will earn points as spelled out for them on a rubric: points for immediately putting the napkin in their lap, points for knowing which fork to use, points for eating slowly and with their mouths closed, points for participating in an enjoyable conversation, and so on. Parents will be the judges, and at the end of the night whoever scores the most points will win something special.

Sooner or later, this trick will rub off on your kids and you won't have to worry about how they'll act when it really matters. Remember to play that Sinatra CD softly in the background while you're dining.

PESTERIZATION

"You can only be young once.
But you can always be immature."
—Dave Barry, Pulitzer Prize–winning American humorist

O K, this is as good a spot as any to coin a term. "Pester-izers" are emotionally immature kids who love to stir up trouble at school with their peers. Usually it's just for entertainment, although at times it might be because they feel jealous or threatened. In any regard, they tend to treat others like objects. It is highly doubtful they realize this, or would ever admit to it. Their constant excuse when told to stop pesterizing is "Jeesh, I was just kidding!" In this way, they are a bit like bullies. While they see nothing wrong in the way they treat others, they scream bloody murder when someone does it to them.

Trick: The Pestering the Pesterizer Program

Use It On: Kids eight to twelve who get suspended from school or kicked off the bus because they purposefully bug other kids.

When to Employ: Once you have a stack of teacher complaints, or referrals to in-school suspension, or you realize that no other kids want to play with your kid.

What You'll Need: If your fingers work, you can do this.

The Pestering Program is a procedure that offers pesterizers a classic taste of their own medicine. I used it on an exceptionally bright fifth grader who got bored in his talented and gifted classes and had to stir things up to keep himself entertained. He liked to poke the kids around him or pull at their clothing or hair. His favorite thing was to grab someone's pen, take it apart, and hand it back in pieces. This always cracked him up. His peers were less than amused, as was his teacher.

Here's what we did: I explained to him that kids who bug other kids as much as he did don't usually understand what it feels like, because they don't have anyone doing it to them. So, in order for him to come to full consciousness, we would be forced to give him a small taste of his own medicine. I asked his parents to spend a fair amount of time on Saturday morning poking him, pulling his hair, ears, nose, or clothing, turning off the TV when he was watching it, untying his shoes, giving him a Wet Willy, and so on. I also told his parents to be sure to laugh while doing this, as if it was all just fun and games.

It didn't take long for him to understand what it felt like to be on the receiving end. Some of these pestering children actually assume that other kids *like* to be teased by them, that they find it funny. The Pestering Program rids them of that notion pretty quickly.

Trick: The Poking Program

Use It On: Kids six to twelve who like to poke others at school or on the bus.

When to Employ: As above, once the school complaints pile up.

What You'll Need: Your child will need but one functioning finger. (Preferably not the middle one.)

Speaking of the pesterizer, there's another variation to this trick I used with a compact, good-natured third grader. Even though he was considerably smaller than most of the other boys his age, once you got to know him it was clear that he was a force for his peers to reckon with because he was strong, quick, and athletic. He was smart as well, and a poker to boot. I got the impression he poked others not simply because he was impulsive and bored in the classroom, but because it was also his way of establishing dominance—a juvenile case of short-man syndrome.

Over the period of a month, his mother received an escalating and threatening series of complaints from his school. Her breaking point came when she was told he was about to get kicked out of his after-school program due to his jabbing and poking. She was single, and like a lot of single moms could not afford to continue to leave work and go pick him up due to his behavior.

I told him we would have to put him on a Poking Program to drain all of the poking out of his system. Given it was only his mom and him at the house, and his mom certainly didn't want to be poked, he would have to poke himself for ten minutes nightly until he stopped poking others.

His initial response, due to being a bit oppositional, was that it was no big deal. When kids respond this way, I sometimes say we will have to give them an immediate two-minute taste of what the program would be like, so I asked him to poke himself while I timed him with my stopwatch.

It's amazing just how long two minutes can feel when you're poking yourself, particularly when I let the stopwatch run for three minutes and insist it's only two. He complained and complained about how *loooong* this was taking and how very *stooopid* it was. He started poking himself on his left arm, moved to his chest, went down to his stomach, back up his arm, and so on. Once his time was up, I asked him to imagine how it would be to actually do it for ten minutes. I also had him ask his mother if she really would follow through if he did not knock it off at school. She assured him she would.

When I saw him a couple of weeks after this, I asked how the Poking Program was going. He got a big smile on his face and said "What Poking Program, Dr. Riley? I stopped poking kids a long time ago!"

REGARDING
CELL PHONES

"I don't answer the phone. I get the feeling
whenever I do that there will be someone on the other end."
—*Fred Couples, American golfer*

Arguing with teenagers about cell phones occupies an astonishing amount of time in many families. It used to be that only kids sixteen and up would have cell phones, and then only for emergencies or to get ahold of their parents. With the advent of texting, third graders are now demanding and getting their own phones and their own accounts, just because they want them. Too often I've found that children who are doing the worst at home and at school are allowed privileges that should be accessed only through successful behavior and accomplishment.

In general, I advise parents not to get phones for children younger than fourteen. Once the child has a cell phone, however, there is nothing wrong with using it for leverage. If his or her grades or behavior aren't good enough, *take the thing away*! When I say things like this in my office, the sense of panic on the parent's face is palpable. It's as if parents fear their child will no longer like them if they act like parents. Cell phones are a good idea gone wrong, as we will see in the following scenarios.

Trick: Your Cell Phone Is Broken

Use It On: Kids of any age who have cell phones but won't answer your calls.

When to Employ: When you're finally tired of leaving voice messages along the lines of "This is your mom (or dad). Answer your phone, dammit!"

What You'll Need: A safe place to store your kid's cell phone.

You pay loads of money for your kids' cell phone each month, so why is it you can never get hold of them? The answer, of course, is well known to many tweens and most teens: when your caller ID says it's the "rents," just ignore the call.

The fix for this is quite simple. Tell your child to hand over the phone. Say it's obviously not working, because you can never reach her on it. (It's highly doubtful she'll reply, "That's because I just ignore you when you call.") She'll try to come up with some excuse, like every time you call she's out of range, or something like that. Just tell her you intend to take her phone in to the phone store for repair, and make a big deal about how resentful you are for paying so much for something that doesn't even work. Then, turn her phone off and put it in your purse or the glove box of your car or your desk drawer at work and let it sit for two weeks. Every day when your child asks if her phone is fixed yet, tell her it should be ready soon, but also say, "You know how phone companies are. Takes 'em forever."

When you finally return the phone, tell her to charge it up. After it's charged, take out your own phone and call her number, demonstrating that her phone now works as it should. Tell her if it "breaks" again, you will be more than happy to take it back for further repair.

Trick: Texting Maniac

Use It On: Kids who text but don't turn in homework.

When to Employ: When there is a statistically significant inverse relationship between the frequency of text messaging on the part of your child and his or her grade point average. (In other words, she texts tons, but her grades stink.)

What You'll Need: An actual printout of all the calls and texts your child made in one billing period. Get ready to gasp.

As I write this section, the current record for text messages sent and received by any of the kids I work with is 24,500 in one month. Do the math. That's over *eight hundred* per day! Fifty per hour based on sixteen waking hours per day! Almost one per minute! While this is unusual, it's nothing for me to hear stories of kids sending and receiving over 5,000 text messages per month.

Part of this trick involves sitting down with your child and reviewing just how many messages she's sending and receiving on a daily basis. The reason you need the paper printout is that it makes it really clear that things have gotten out of hand, at least to you, if not to your child.

After doing this, tell your child if she can send/receive hundreds (perhaps thousands) of text messages per month, it gives you great relief along four important lines: (1) it demonstrates she knows how to read, (2) it demonstrates she knows how to write, and (3) it demonstrates she knows how to get messages delivered to the appropriate person in a timely manner. Therefore, (4) there will no longer be any excuses for schoolwork and homework not being written, completed, and handed in on time. If the grades remain poor, bye-bye, cell phone.

Trick: The Shortest Trick in the Book

Use It On: Elementary school student who says things to you like "Emily's parents gave her one. They must love her more than you love me."

When to Employ: When it's obvious your child is trying to guilt-trip you into getting her a cell phone.

What You'll Need: Parental attitude.

This is what to say to your elementary school child when she insists that she *needs* a cell phone: "Ha ha. Ha ha ha ha ha."

SLOW-POKEY KIDS

"Anyone who thinks the art of conversation
is dead ought to tell a child to go to bed."
—*Robert Gallagher, English photographer*

The cure for people who are pathologically punctual is to have kids. Having kids will cure you of any delusions you have about being on time. Who knows why kids are so slow. Maybe they're just not wired to move fast unless they're chasing the brother or sister who made them mad. Maybe they're just too easily distracted, and our agenda falls out of the forefront of their thinking because they're watching the fan go round and round, or they spotted a ladybug crawling up the wall. But as every parent knows, there are times when the wait is intolerable. It's neither sweet nor funny when your boss is yelling at you for being late again. There's nothing pleasant about the principal staring at you

172

over her glasses, arms crossed and tapping her foot as you drag your kid screaming toward his classroom five minutes after the bell has rung. Is this the life you're leading? If so, give some of these tricks a try.

Trick: Stop and Go

Use It On: Kids six to twelve who make you late (not to mention make you *crazy*).

When to Employ: After even your best friends at work start to complain about your tardiness.

What You'll Need: Visual distractions in your neighborhood; cool new places to check out while you drive.

Does your child always keep you waiting? Here's something you might try: the next time she needs to be somewhere on time (field hockey practice, for example), tell her to get in the car and buckle up. Drive about ten feet, then announce that you forgot something. Tell her to stay buckled, turn off the car, take the keys with you, and go back into the house. Sit down and read a magazine for five minutes, and then get back into the car. Pull out of your driveway, go another ten feet, and stop the car to admire the neighbor's flowers or landscaping. After she begins to grumble, drive in the direction you typically would take to get to her destination. Drive extra slow. Stop to get a bottle of water at a convenience store. When she finally starts to complain about how late she's going to be and how irritating it has been to be kept waiting and how mad her coach is going to be, pull over. You've now got her where you want her. Tell her it's time for the two of you to make a deal . . .

Trick: Butler's Salary

Use It On: Kids age six to nine who take their good sweet time while getting dressed.

When to Employ: After your child has made you late for that meeting you had with your boss to discuss why you deserve a raise.

What You'll Need: Your child will need some money, and you'll need a list of jobs that need to be done.

Do you have a young child who just won't get dressed in the morning? Is your frustrated solution to yell or shout? Shouting, as they say, has become the new spanking in many families.

There's a better way. The next time your child is about to make you late, tell her you're going to take control of getting her dressed and she'll no longer have to worry about this particular chore until she is older. However, tell her you intend to charge her fifty cents every time you dress her, and you will be the one to choose what she wears.

And how is she to come by this sum of money? Assure her it will not be had easily, as in paying you from her allowance, or paying you with money she got from the tooth fairy. No, she will have to pay you with money she has *earned*. Tell her that as long as you are forced to be her dresser, you'll have a list of chores waiting for her every day when she gets home from school. It will be from this income that she will purchase your dressing services. Of course, you'll need to toss in there somewhere that she always has the option to dress herself for free *anytime she wants.*

Trick: The Funky Outfit

Use It On: Peter Pan kids, six to nine, the ones who don't want to grow up.

When to employ: When your school-age child actually wants you to dress her.

What You'll Need: A random assortment of your child's clothing.

OK, suppose your child actually likes it when you dress her. Some children have periods of regression in which they want to be treated like a baby again. When asked to get dressed for school they might even say in a singsongy voice, "Me too little. Dress me, Mommy."

If your child goes through this not-uncommon phase, don't waste too many mornings arguing with her to get herself dressed. Instead, get yourself dressed for the day, have some breakfast, and when there are only five minutes left before your daughter has to meet the bus or you have to be on the road to school, rush her into the bedroom and begin putting her outfit together. Don't spend too much time making it match, either. In fact, throw in an item of clothing you know your child doesn't like to begin with. Watch your child's face as you hurriedly put together something mildly strange and unexpected.

I will never forget what one little patient said regarding her mother's use of this trick: "She made me wear something *funky!*" As with this child, the combination of hurried dressing along with the haphazard choice of clothing may be enough to make your little one ditch the idea of being dressed by Mommy.

Trick: The Thirty-Second Solution

Use It On: Older kids, ten to fourteen, who take forever to choose their outfits and get dressed.

When to Employ: When you want to save time, as well as money.

What You'll Need: Hopefully you like khakis.

Here's another trick to consider if you have a child in the ten- to fourteen-year-old range who takes forever to get dressed, making *her* late for school and *you* late for work. It's similar to the Victim of Capitalism (page 51) and Fashion Feng Shui tricks (page 54).

Just as in these tricks, you'll need to apologize for giving her too many clothing choices. Tell her you overdid it, not realizing that giving her so many clothes would make it impossible for her to make a decision about what to wear to school.

Tell her you intend to reduce her school wardrobe down to a "uniform" of two pairs of khaki pants (one dark blue, one tan) and two polo shirts (one medium blue, one white). Explain that this will totally eliminate her "choice confusion" in the morning.

Plus, point out the *main* advantage of wearing a uniform: due to the fact that her pants and shirts are the same cut, the magic of muscle memory will take over quickly and getting dressed will be as fast and easy as falling off the proverbial log. She'll be able to do it in thirty seconds with her eyes closed (which is probably a good thing, given how awake she is for the first hour she's up). As usual, tell her you're totally serious about this solution, given all the time and money it would save you. However, if you see rapid changes, you won't have to use tricks like this at all.

TOUCHY KIDS
AND FIT THROWERS

"People who fly into a rage always make a bad landing."
—*Will Rogers*

Some kids have a sort of built-in touchiness to them. They scream bloody murder if anyone bumps into them, or they melt down in the car if you stop somewhere unanticipated. They make you want to pull your hair out because their overreaction to small things leaves you both angry at them in the moment and frightened for them in the long run. While it is certainly smart to think about a pediatric consult for these children, here are some tricks that I've used quite successfully.

Trick: Bump Training

Use It On: Kids (typically boys), age six to ten, who are so physically or emotionally brittle that they think they ought to be taken to the school nurse or the emergency room every time someone bumps into them.

When to Employ: When you give your child a playful poke and he falls down like he's been shot, or yells at you for trying to maim him.

What You'll Need: Forearms.

If you have a child who screams bloody murder every time someone bumps into him just a little bit, you might want to talk to his pediatrician about sensory processing disorder. Kids with this can sometimes be exquisitely sensitive to bumps, bangs, tags in their shirts, lines on the toes of their socks, and so on. But if it's not SPD, just your kid being overly sensitive, think about giving him some bump training: every time you walk by him, bump him with your forearm, making sure to add "Boom!" or "Bang!" or "Whack!" or some other sound effect. He'll hate it at first and will probably accuse you to trying to hurt him. But invite him to do the same to you and pretty soon he'll be over his sensitivity. An added bonus: he'll be able to put up with all the bumping and banging and pushing and shoving that's part of the guy world, and thus won't be so easily rejected by the other boys.

Trick: Mistake Training

Use It On: Kids six to ten who are fearful of making mistakes.

When To Employ: If you happen to be close to your child when she makes some small mistake and you see her eyes widen with fear like Bambi caught in your headlights, and she breaks down crying hysterically or throws a fit.

What You'll Need: Paper cups, an egg, and two very old shirts.

We don't want our kids to be afraid of their mistakes. If they grow up being afraid of making mistakes, they'll never try anything new. So, our job is to teach kids to say the following when they make the typical childhood gaffe: "That's no big deal. I'll just fix it (or clean it up)." To do this, take a deep breath if you're an anxious adult and do the following:

For five nights in a row, make sure your child knocks over a cup of water during dinner. Have her say her mantra while she cleans up the mess.

If you have resilient flooring in your kitchen, have your child drop an egg. Have her say her mantra as she cleans it up. If it's a big mess, so what? It just teaches her that it really is no big deal.

Take her to a fast-food joint, both of you being sure to wear old shirts. Order a sandwich of some sort and douse it in ketchup. Lean back when you eat it so you can get ketchup all over your shirt. When you get home, repeat the mantra while you rub stain remover onto the spots and toss the shirt into the washing machine.

If your child remains fearful of her mistakes after this, repeat all procedures again for a second week, being sure to laugh as much as possible. Don't be like the mom who got so nervous when I started talking about these tricks that she had to leave the room.

Trick: Switch It Up

Use It On: Children six and up who are developing an obsessive need to keep everything the same.

When to employ: After your child starts to scream at you for taking a different route to the mall, or demands that dinner be served at exactly the same time every night, or flips out if anyone changes the order of the plush toys on her bed.

What You'll Need: Freedom from OCD yourself.

If you see your child acting the way I described above, what you're seeing is the thin edge of the wedge of obsessive compulsive disorder, and you better go ahead and disrupt its development *right now*. Do not let your child fall into believing that everything is predictable and that everything will stay the same. You'll need to build some resilience into her system by having her encounter unexpected changes and unexpected events. Does she demand you drive the same way to school every day? Take a new route. Does she insist snacks come before bath time? Switch it to afterward. Tell her you're going to the grocery store. Then detour to the hardware store. Have her trade chairs at the dinner table with her brother. Will she protest loudly? Guaranteed. But will she be a happier person once she learns to deal gracefully with life's unpredictable events? Also guaranteed.

Trick: But I'm Siii-iiick!

Use It On: Young hypochondriacs, six to twelve, who call you from the nurse's office demanding to be taken home due to illness but who never give you the satisfaction of actually throwing up or running a fever.

When to Employ: When you have no sick days left for yourself because you've used them all up going to school to get your "sick" child.

What You'll Need: A wiring diagram of your house.

If you have a child you're tempted to use this trick on, do remain aware of the possibility of underlying issues. Some kids try to escape school because they're fearful of certain subjects or certain teachers. Sometimes they're fearful of other kids, or they're developing social anxiety and want to isolate themselves. But most often they're just tired of school and would rather come home and play.

I knew a mom whose son called her once per week at work, like clockwork, to come get him from the nurse's office. When she would question him about his symptoms or cast any doubt whatsoever on his illness, he would scream at her over the phone, "But I'm siii-iiick!" Sometimes she would refuse to go get him, but most times she did. She couldn't help but notice that within an hour of being home he was well enough to watch TV or play video games.

Here's what we did. The next time he called, she rushed right to the school to get him. She announced on the ride home that she intended to take his illness very seriously. She would get him to bed quickly, making sure his curtains were drawn and his room was dark so he could rest. She told him he could not turn on his lights, TV, or PlayStation. If he did, she would turn off the electrical breaker to his room and he would have no electricity in there at all. He was to stay in bed for the rest of the afternoon, evening, and into the next morning. She would bring him a cup of chicken noodle soup for dinner, and he would eat it in bed. She indicated that she would take every opportunity available to feel his forehead for the rest of the week, because as sick as he was it was highly likely that he would have to go straight to bed after school on Friday, and remain there until Monday morning.

Let's put it this way: the more his mother demonstrated over the next few weeks just how intent she was on taking care of him, the better he felt.

Trick: The Little Kid Program

Use It On: Big-time fit throwers, five to nine.

When to Employ: When you just can't take one more of those massive meltdowns that your child is treating you to on an increasingly frequent basis.

What You'll Need: A strong stomach, because you don't want to threaten using this trick if you're not willing to follow through. You'll also need a Teletubbies DVD.

Here's a trick for kids five to nine who have become kindergarten or early elementary legends because of their tantrums. This is the hot jalapeno, the Naga Jolokia, the ghost chili of tricks. Use it sparingly, *only* when all other techniques have failed, and *only* when both parents are in agreement that it should be used. And this is one of those points in the book where you absolutely have to return to the end of Chapter 1 and re-read the rules on when not to use tricks (page 15). If your child is developmentally challenged or on the autistic spectrum, is anxious or depressed, is mean-minded, or bullies others, do *not* use the Little Kid Program. It is for normal, average kids who objectively have no problems other than the fact that they throw huge fits.

You'll need to talk to your child at a calm moment. Sit down with him and say that the next time he throws a massive fit, he'll be placed on the Little Kid Program. The premise of the program is simple: act big, get treated big; act little, get treated little. As usual, offer your child the soft landing: if he ceases the massive tantrums, there will be no need for such tricks at your house.

Here are the rules for the twenty-four-hour period following a monstrous fit:

- Bedtime is 6:30 P.M.
- The only television or videos that can be watched prior to bedtime are Teletubbies DVDs. If your child likes those, then no videos at all. You can find them on Amazon, and elsewhere.
- The only toys that can be played with once the child returns home from school the next day (or all day long if he or she is receiving the consequences during the weekend) are two Legos or two blocks. Nothing else. Video games, computers, TV, and anything else with electrons is strictly forbidden until your child is back in the Big Kid Zone.
- A little kid dinner (lunch too, if it's a weekend) is always the same: a hot dog that has been heated and cut up into itty-bitty pieces to be eaten with the fingers (nothing to dip it in—would be too messy), a piece of American cheese cut up into itty-bitty pieces, and a pickle cut up into itty-bitty pieces (this meal is based on what my kids loved to eat when they were three). And you get a cup of milk or juice in a sippy cup.

- A little kid breakfast is always the same: a frozen waffle, heated up, no syrup, no jelly, no butter, no nothing, cut up into itty-bitty pieces to be eaten with the fingers and, of course, a cup of milk or juice in a sippy cup.

Will your fit thrower begin to display more self-control simply by being told you will use this trick? In most cases, absolutely, because it is such strong medicine and illustrates so dramatically that Mom and Dad are no longer going to put up with out-of-control behavior. If you have to follow through, a day on the Little Kid Program is not something your child will be likely to forget anytime soon.

GROSS STUFF

"The hardest job kids face today is
learning good manners without seeing any."
—*Fred Astaire, American dancer and actor*

E ver feel like you're living in ancient Rome, right about the time the barbarians were getting ready to sack the place? Do you feel like you're trying your hardest to keep things civilized, but your son, Alaric the First, king of the Visigoths, doesn't seem to be picking up on the fact that mastering certain types of personal manners makes life a whole lot more pleasant for the people who have to live with him? If so, I have a couple of tricks for you.

Trick: Can't Remember to Flush the Potty

Use It On: Boys six to ten who don't seem to understand the function of that handle thingy on the side of the toilet.

When to Employ: Once you're tired of walking into the bathroom, only to find a horrible surprise waiting for you.

What You'll Need: A functioning toilet.

If you have a husband or other appropriate male role model to turn to, tell him you need his help. Here's what he will have to explain to your son: "One of the first steps along the road to becoming a civilized man is learning how to flush a toilet. It doesn't matter one nit that the vast majority of males don't know how to flush a toilet, as can easily be witnessed by going into the men's room at any gas station, sports arena, or restaurant. It's now time for *you* to learn this important cultural skill."

As with many of the other tricks in the box, employing repetition can work wonders in helping hardheaded children acquire new skills. Have your husband or role model explain to your son that the only way for him to acquire any new skill is to practice it over and over until it has been mastered. Tell the young man that he is not to do anything else while he practices, like listen to his iPod or send text messages, because this would be much too distracting. He will simply have to stand there while the bowl refills after each and every flush, and then push the lever again.

Offer him the soft landing: flush the toilet after you're finished with your business, and no tricks will be necessary. If not, practice can begin any day. Fathers and role models: if the young man has been cooperative and seems to have some insight into the issue, take him out to lunch and have a friendly talk about the other kinds of things a man needs to learn to do in order to become a civilized male. Truth be told, he will probably enjoy the attention.

Trick: Burps and Farts

Use It On: Six- to ten-year-old boys who like to entertain others with their private noises.

When to Employ: Once it's obvious that nobody but them thinks it's funny.

What You'll Need: Earplugs, room freshener, and a straight face. Your sons will provide all the necessary sound effects and odors.

Boys who are too old to be thought of as "little" but too young to be interested in girls like to burp and fart. You need to accept this and move on. They're immature and will grow out of it, unless, of course, they grow up to be men who still like to burp and fart. If you're married to a grown man who still thinks it's cute to burp and fart, this trick will be of little help to you.

So, back to the boys. If you live with a burper and/or farter, stay focused on the idea that he's immature. That means that if you try to talk with him seriously about his habit, chances are he'll get so caught up in giggling about the subject that he won't be able to stop giggling. But you can rest assured that he'll sneak a burp or a fart in there somewhere.

The better way to deal with this issue is to use a draining procedure, in which you insist that he burp and fart repeatedly, over and over for the next half hour in order to get all the burps and farts out of his system. As with any of these types of programs, tell your son if he continues to grace you with these lovely noises after you had him do it for half an hour, the next time will be for forty-five minutes. This trick worked wonders for a mother whose son, during dinner, liked to proudly show off his ability to sing the first few bars of "The Star Spangled Banner" by burping.

INTERRUPTERS AND SUBJECT SHIFTERS

"Listen or thy tongue will keep thee deaf."
—Indian proverb

There are two main types of interrupters, as far as I can tell: one type is totally locked in to what you are saying but wants so desperately to be part of the conversation that he or she talks right over you. The other type will look at you and nod and make it seem like he's hearing everything you say. Then, when you pause, he will say something so far removed from what you were talking about that you realize he was totally tuned out all along.

The upside is that at least these kids want to talk to adults and share their thoughts. The downside, of course, is that their communication patterns can be pretty irritating, and they may end up alienating their peers and teachers. So, our job is to help them understand what effect they have on others with the way they communicate.

Trick: Conversus Interruptus

Use It On: Children, six to fourteen, who constantly interrupt you during conversations, regardless of the fact that you have asked them over and over not to do so.

When to Employ: When it becomes clear that the only words you can get in are the edgewise ones.

What You'll Need: A humorous desire to show your child what constantly being interrupted feels like.

I use this trick on occasion at my office when it becomes evident that a child has an interrupting problem. It is important to note that interrupters generally have no idea whatsoever of their impact on others. Because of this, they need to be shown by offering them a gentle taste of their own medicine.

This is how you can do it at home: first, explain to your child that for the next few minutes you will be engaged in a conversation about a topic you know to be of interest to her. Warn her, however, that after every five words or so that come out of her mouth, you are going to butt in with your own ideas. Tell her that it is not being done to be mean or vengeful, but simply to show her how irritating it is to try to talk to an interrupter.

Then start the conversation. After each interruption, make sure you ask a question or prompt your child to say something else so the conversation will continue, and so you can interrupt again.

If your child refuses to go along with this role-play but continues to interrupt you or talk over you, you will be forced to do your interrupting during real conversations. Will your child get irritated with you? Absolutely. However, it gives you the perfect opportunity to talk to her about the negative impact that interrupting has on people. Do this frequently enough and your interrupter will learn a valuable lesson.

Trick: Shifting the Subject

Use It On: Children six to fourteen who change subjects out of the blue during conversation.

When to Employ: When it's evident that your child is not really listening—which is the real reason he shifts subjects to begin with.

What You'll Need: A mental list of *weird* subjects to shift into at the drop of a hat.

Have you heard of shape shifters, those mythical creatures that change form at will? Some kids are like this when it comes to talk. They will transmogrify the conversation in an instant. You'll be talking to them about what time you need to pick them up at school for their doctor's appointment, and they'll look at you blankly and respond by telling you about the yo-yo some kid brought to school that day.

There's a game I play with kids who do this. First, I put four quarters on my desk. Next, I tell them we're going to have a conversation and somewhere along the line I'm going to do a "switch." For example, we might be talking about their favorite movie, and without warning I'll start talking about what kind of bugs trout like to eat in the spring. If they can catch me switching, I'll give them a quarter.

They catch me often, and get a kick out of winning the quarter. More often, however, they do not. The most inattentive children will fail to realize I made a switch and will just follow right along as I shift the subject all over the place. At such times I point out I just made a switch, and put one of the quarters into my pocket. We keep the game going until the quarters are gone. Kids usually gain some insight from this and enjoy it thoroughly.

I also tell parents to do something similar at home, particularly when the child is making a request. This seems to really get the child's attention and makes him work harder on being aware of his own switches.

Child: "Mom, I got invited to go to the movies with Justin tonight. Can I go?"

You: "What movie are you going to go see?"

Child: "The new movie about mummies."

You: "That sounds just like something up your alley. Pretty scary, I bet."

Child: "So can I go?"

You: "Sometimes I like blue cheese dressing on my salad. Other times oil and vinegar tastes just fine."

Child: "Mom!"

You: "What?—did I get off subject or something?"

Child: "Yeah. I was talking about a movie, and you started talking about salad dressing. For no reason."

You: "OK, movies . . . What movies?"

Child: "The one about mummies! I already told you that."

You: "Oh! Yeah! I need to stop by the cleaners this morning to pick up your dad's suit. He got a stain on it that looks like a profile of Abraham Lincoln's face."

Child: "Mom! Mom! Earth to Mom! Pay attention!"

Eventually your little shifter will come to recognize when he or others are shifting the subject. Be patient with him, while at the same time using humor and good-natured feedback to help him lose this habit.

WORRYWARTS

*"Don't tell me that worry doesn't do any good.
I know better. The things I worry about don't happen."*
—*Anonymous*

You need big tricks for little worriers, particularly if they've begun to keep you up all night with their fears and nightmares. It's too easy to fall into thinking that just because the things that scare children at night seem so cartoonish, we can dismiss their fright as also not being real. For the child, there's no safety to be found in such a solution. Instead, we need to give children new ways to think about bad dreams and monsters, and new ways to respond. See if the following tricks offer your little worrier a bit of relief, and improve your sleep as well.

Trick: Stupid Vampires

Use It On: Children age six to nine who are afraid to go to sleep at night because they're convinced their bedrooms are populated by monsters, ghosts, spookies, vampires, zombies, Chuckie, Freddy Krueger, and all manner of other bad-to-the-bone creatures.

When to Employ: Know how you can't get enough sleep because your kids end up in your bed and their little elbows dig into your ribs or they smack you in the face every time they roll over or worse yet, you wake up wet and warm? That's when you use this trick.

What You'll Need: A vampire IQ test would be helpful.

Every parent has been through this scenario. Their child is terrified to be in his or her bedroom alone out of fear of being captured and hauled away and tortured or eaten. Scary stuff for sure when you look at it through a child's eyes. Sit down with your child and have the following conversation:

Parent: "You still afraid of vampires getting you at night?"

Child: "Yeah, sorta."

Parent: "How often do you think vampires come into your room?"

Child: "Lots. Every night."

Parent: "So how many times have they really managed to get you and take you away? I don't mean in your dreams or imagination. How many times have they really captured you?"

Child: "Uh, none, I guess."

Parent: "So they come into your room a lot but they never manage to find you?"

Child: "I guess not."

Parent: "Then they must be really stupid."

Child: "What?"

Parent: "Well, they roam around your room all night, from what you tell me, but it's never occurred to them to look under the covers to find you. So they must be really stupid."

Child: "Ha ha! Yeah, I never thought about it like that."

Parent: "Or maybe it means they aren't real to begin with. What do you think?"

Have this discussion with your child on a nightly basis. Your child is going to be pretty skeptical at first, but soon it will dawn on him or her that vampires aren't real. After that, you'll be safe to make jokes about just how stupid all monsters are because you've never seen a real news report about a real kid being kidnapped by a real monster.

Trick: Braveheart

Use It On: Children six to eight (or a little older) who are fearful of going into certain rooms or areas of your house alone.

When to employ: If your child won't go upstairs without you, or insists that you go with her into her room, or will not go to the bathroom unless you stand right outside the door, or will not let you go to the bathroom unless *she* stands right outside the door.

What You'll Need: Quarters and a stopwatch.

It's not unusual for children to be afraid of certain areas of your house. However, we don't want them to be ruled by their fears. If this is the case at your house, try this: teach your child how to start your stopwatch, let it run for two minutes, and then pause it. After she knows how to work the watch, put four quarters on the table. Tell her that the way to win a quarter is to go into, say, an upstairs bedroom she's hesitant about, stay in there for two minutes, and then come back down and show you the watch. Then she gets to do it three more times, ideally choosing a different scary room or area each time and ultimately earning one dollar. Play this game every night for a week. Chances are if you can get her to venture into frightening rooms or other scary areas of your house repeatedly, she'll lose her fear of those spaces.

An alternative: some kids are simply fascinated with the stopwatch and with timing themselves, and will go into various scary rooms without needing any money as an inducement. But don't forget to offer praise and hugs.

Trick: Dreamweavers

Use It On: Kids ten and younger who run screaming into your bedroom because some thirty-foot-tall green, slimy thing with six yellow eyes was about to bite them.

When to Employ: When your child comes into your room so often that the slime monster is wrecking your sleep too.

What You'll Need: Laser-beam eyeballs.

If your child is waking you up often with her bad dreams, here's a trick I teach to lots of parents and kids. At bedtime each night, lie down with your child and talk to her about the kind of dreams she would like to have. Be sure to invite her to add all the silly, phantasmagorical details she can imagine. Tell her when you turn out the lights and close her door, she should continue to pretend she's asleep and having her wonderful dream.

But if she still wakes up frightened and comes into your room? Have her sit with you and close her eyes so that she can redo her dream. This time, when the slime monster is chasing her, have her use her laser-beam eyeballs to heat him up and watch him explode. BOOM! Monster guts and slime and eyeballs all over the place! Or, if she prefers, she can use her laser-beam eyeballs to shrink the slime monster down to one inch tall. Tell her that you'd like her to learn how to redo her dreams right there in her room when she wakes up frightened.

As one boy told me at my office, "I'd shrink him and then I'd put him in my pocket and keep him for a pet."

Trick: Nail Biters

Use It On: Girls six to ten who bite their nails to the quick.

When to Employ: When their nails are mangled and their little fingers are red and sore from all the biting and picking.

What You'll Need: Nail polish. Your daughter gets to choose the color.

Sometimes worries don't just express themselves in dreams. Sometimes worried children bite their nails. At my office, any girl with fingers like the ones I described above who goes without biting her nails for one month gets to paint my nails any color she likes: sparkle polish, multiple colors, faces, rainbows, whatever. I have to wear it all day long.

OK, dads and other significant males: time to step up to the plate and show your pride in your girl's accomplishment.

THE BIGGEST
TRICK IN THE BOX

"The first duty of love is to listen."
—*Paul Tillich, German-born American theologian and philosopher*

If you want to see the biggest trick of all, go look in the mirror. In particular, look at those two things protruding from either side of your head—your ears. They are not there to serve as radiators to cool your blood, as with rabbits. They were not put there during the evolution or creation process simply to be used as jewelry hangers. No, bringing peace and harmony to your home will not be hard work at all as long as you use your ears for their intended purpose. This means sitting with your children on a regular basis and listening to their fantasies about what and how and who they want to be. This means listening deeply.

This deep listening is a process I've referred to over the years and in my other writing as "the fascinated ear." It is the missing link for most parents and their children. I've found over and over in my work with children that once listening is restored, things invariably get better. The reason for this? Children have a way of knowing if they have your rapt attention, or if you're just listening with a small percentage of your ability while your mind is off on other things. From my perspective, children have a right to *all* of your attention for at least a brief period of time every day, because it's through talking to you that they clarify who they are and who they will become as individuals. You don't feel validated as a human being until at least one other person in your life seems to understand you, and nods and demonstrates that he or she can see the world through your eyes.

What can we do to demonstrate this fascinated ear to our children? There are any number of ways, some of them quite simple, others requiring a bit more effort. For example, if you're busy at your kitchen counter or work bench and your child comes to you with a question, make sure that you put down what you're doing, make eye contact, and try to address whatever issue it is he or she brings up. I know, I know, boy, do I ever know—there are some kids who will go on and on and on once they have your attention, and it is OK to encourage them to get to the point. But you must do this kindly, and with your full attention turned in their direction.

There are other ways to use the fascinated ear as well: turn off the TV at mealtimes and eat together whenever possible. And tell your teenagers to turn off their cell phones during dinner, as those urgent text messages about who just broke up with whom can wait. Quality time together, as a family, cannot wait.

My favorite method, however, for parents to demonstrate a fascinated ear comes in the form of "boy's night out" and "girl's night out." Ideally, whether you are a mother or father, at least once a month, you and your child should get into your vehicle and go out to breakfast, lunch, or dinner—just the two of you. It does not have to be anything fancy—tacos, burgers, or pizza will do just fine.

Here are the ground rules: boy's night out/girl's night out has one purpose, and one purpose only. It gives you time with your son or daughter that is specifically meant for listening to them talk about *their* world—what *they* are interested in being one day, who *they* are hanging out with, what music *they* like on the radio, what movie or book has *their* attention, and so on. This is not a time in which any correcting or wagging of fingers is allowed, because doing so in this atmosphere will shut things down faster than pushing the big red button at a nuclear power plant. And it is certainly not a time to demonstrate your intellectual superiority or a time for all those "yeah buts."

You know what I'm talking about. I'll never forget an incident in my office with a six-year-old boy whose father was in jail. He picked up a small model of a Porsche I had on my desk, enclosed in a little see-through box—a Christmas present from another boy who knew I was a car nut. "Wow," he told me. "This car costs three million dollars and goes three hundred miles an hour!"

"Those are cool cars," I remember saying. "But they don't cost quite that much. This type costs about seventy thousand, and will go about a hundred and seventy-five."

It was like letting all the air out of a balloon. He set the car back down and looked away. There would have been plenty of chances later on to educate him a little more realistically about sticker price and top speed. But I missed the opportunity to engage him in a discussion of cars that are wicked fast and crazy expensive. I missed the opportunity to talk with him about things that are larger than life and of absolutely mythical proportion, something all children love.

When I talk to many well-meaning parents about the concept of spending time with their children, they assure me that they already do. I was talking to a dad at my office recently about this very topic because his son had complained to me that he and his dad never did anything together. His dad's response was that he didn't know what his son was talking about because he spent *lots* of quality time with his son. He told me that when he made his inevitable Saturday morning run to Lowes or Home Depot, he *always* took his son with him, and they usually stopped to get a snack or a treat along the way. He said he used going into these stores as a way to teach his son how various tools and implements are used in building and maintaining a home.

I agreed with him that all of this is noble. Dads need to teach their sons how to use tools to build and repair things, in my viewpoint, because it's a type of mentoring that helps boys become masters of their own universe. However well intentioned, this father entirely missed the point. His son would tell you that his dad never spent any time doing things with him that *he* liked. His dad only spent time with him doing things that his dad liked.

Let's not jump on this dad too fast. He was obviously trying to do the right thing, and obviously thinking about his son's needs. Where his viewpoint diverged from the viewpoint underlying the theory of the fascinated ear is that children don't measure how much time you spend with them by how long it takes to get to where you are going, or by how long you are together while running errands. In a child's mind, time spent together is measured by how much time you spend doing something the child craves doing, or talking about subjects of deep interest to the child—things the parent may not find interesting at all, in truth, but things that light up the child incandescently. With this particular child, I asked him if he and his dad had common interests. His response was "My dad has no idea what I'm into."

I've heard this same complaint from girls too, especially in regard to their fathers. Often, it seems, dads take a hands-off approach when it comes to spending quality time with their daughters. It is almost as if they feel that because they've never been a girl, they can't even begin to understand a girl's feelings or interests—as if girls are a different species altogether. In truth, girls have as many interests and goals as boys do. And girls, being verbal, love nothing more than to talk about them. The girls I see whose fathers take an active interest in the sports they play, the classes they take, the colleges they are interested in, the music they like to listen to, the clothes and makeup they like to wear, are almost always the girls who do not need a boy to complete them.

Fathers should not be afraid to ask their daughters questions, to learn the ins and outs of the girl world. And fathers should not be afraid to teach girls practical things: how to put oil in a car, how to use an electric drill, etc. These things will surely bring fathers and daughters closer together, and will lessen the need for the tricks you see in this book.

One father I know who has young daughters tells me he knows more about Barbies than any male should reasonably be expected to know. He talks at length with his daughters about Barbie accessories, and spends hours with them on the Barbie website. His girls readily seek him out, go fishing with him, and show the same interest in his life that he shows in theirs. I know another father who often wears a pink extreme cheerleading T-shirt. He's clearly proud of his daughter's involvement in this activity. This is the kind of fascinated ear you are after.

Now, if you have more than one child, you may already be muttering over the fact that this will take up lots of nights every month. I can promise you, from the perspective of a dad whose sons are now grown, you will not regret any of the time you spent out alone with them once they are older and gone. Plus, when all is said and done, you'll actually be spending less time arguing over the stupid things because you'll just be getting along *better.* Your child will now be listening to you better. Believe me, you'll wish you had done boy's night out or girl's night out a lot more often.

Let's suppose you put your plan together. You spend the one-on-one time with your child, and you develop a decent knowledge base about his or her interests so the two of you can talk at length during your time together. What's next? As sure as there will be gravity tomorrow, your child's interests are going to change. Somewhere in there, after you have learned most of what there is to know about soccer, or fishing, or BMX bikes, or American Girl cards, or makeup, or whatever, your child will wake up one day and consider these fascinations to now be either passé, or too young for them. You'll have to move on with them.

I certainly had to do this with my own sons. My oldest, at one point, in addition to being a walking encyclopedia about marine life became a car detailing fanatic. He researched every way to clean and wax and polish a car, to the point that any car he had cleaned would be better off used as a museum piece as opposed to being driven on the highway with all the slobs and dirt and grit you'd be sure to encounter. Somewhere in there his interest in cars waned. Always fearless, he bought a Jeep and developed a keen interest in getting a kayak and going fishing for fish roughly the size of his kayak. So now I've had to learn about the various brands of kayaks and the various types, and how one outfits kayaks for camping trips so you can hop from one little barrier island to another, chasing red fish and tarpon. I now have my own kayak, and if you happen to read something in the paper about a psychologist being eaten by a large fish off the coast of Virginia, you will know the background story. To be just a bit more serious, I've enjoyed the changes in subject matter and have been broadened by them. Learning new stuff keeps us close, and it keeps me from getting in a rut.

It has been the same with my youngest son. In high school, he became a demon tennis player. He studied and talked about the styles and techniques of the top professional players, and could tell you all the advantages of serve and volley versus standing and banging from the baseline. He knew every type of spin to put on his serve and forehand. We would talk about these things for hours.

Then, in college he developed a keen interest in jujitsu and martial arts. Because of this, we've spent countless evenings watching and talking about mixed martial arts bouts. One of the most endearing moments of my life was when he turned toward me on the couch one late night and said, "Hey, Dad, do you know how cool it is to have a dad who likes the same stuff I like?" In my head, I thought to myself, *You're damn right I do!* Because of my son, I know the name of every fighter, and sometimes a considerable amount about their background and history. (Did you know that Chuck Liddell, a ferocious former UFC mixed martial arts champion, has a degree in *accounting*?)

But now he's getting ready to launch off into law school, and I'm hearing of a new fascination: alternative dispute resolution, otherwise known as ADR. He's a philosophical young man, a born peacemaker. Will my wife and I follow him into his new obsessions, learning more and more about the history of ADR, and how ADR can be used in private and corporate and diplomatic disputes? Will we peek into his textbooks, hoping to pick up on the language of his new profession? We will, we will. And we will be better off for it in the long run because it will have the dual effect of teaching us things we never dreamed we'd know while keeping us close to him in the process.

EPILOGUE:
A FEW PARTING WORDS

That closeness I just talked about in the last chapter—that's really the key to solving most of the issues that bedevil you as a parent. Of course there are going to be times when you want to scream at your kids when they're driving you up a pole with their arguing and smarty-pants attitude. Any parent who denies this is either lying or is in some odd way measurably different from the rest of the six billion or so other human beings who inhabit this planet. But the more you listen and interact, the closer you'll feel to your children. The closer you feel to them, the more you'll be able to remember that at their most trying moments, when all things are summed, they're just being kids. Kids make you nuts. Kids make you cry. Kids scare the hell out of you. Kids make you proud. We tumble with our children like pebbles in a stream, and in doing so get our corners and edges worn away, ultimately taking on a new shape. Don't delude yourself into thinking that as the parent, you're the one who did all the influencing during your child's formative years. In their own way, your kids turn you into who you end up being.

So here's the parting advice: use those ears. Doing this will decrease conflict. And when your kids do go off the beam and won't listen to talk and reason and logic, rather than yelling and screaming and certainly rather than hitting, try my tricks or tricks you've invented on your own to get them to listen better. Use the tricks kindly, and with humor. Then, when the kids get it right, praise the dickens out of them. Have fun with them, knowing in advance that you'll miss them one day. You're fated, I'll bet, to wish you had listened just a bit more, played just a bit more, told a few more jokes, and had more fun together than you did. Take advantage of the opportunity while you can.

Invent Your Own Tricks and Share Them with Others

As the saying goes, necessity is the mother of invention. If you invent some tricks of your own and they work particularly well, I'd like to hear about them. I intend to update this book from time to time, and in future editions will add tricks invented by parents. You'll get credit for your invention, not to mention being able to brag to your friends that you've been published. Please contact me through my website: drdouglasriley.com.

ACKNOWLEDGMENTS

This book is the end result of collaborations, both planned and unplanned, with a group of people I am grateful to be able to thank publically.

My partner in this enterprise has always been my wife, Debra Lintz-Riley. She and I have obsessed about "tricks" for over a decade. We looked forward to road trips because they provided us with those rare times when our kids were asleep, we were both awake, and we could jabber on about a topic we loved—how to remove yelling, screaming, and arguing from parenting. We had the idea that there had to be a better way to get a child's attention than volume and time out and takeaways. We wanted to find a way to add humor and lightness, but in a way that would grab a child's attention. What you have here is the best of our late night ramblings.

I have angels watching over me. My late mentor, Dr. Robert Betz, and my late colleague, Dr. Tom Lanning, were not men who could easily exist within the stuffy confines of overly serious academic psychology. When they laughed, they roared. When they joked, they were not always polite. If this book makes you smile, thank them both. And be sure to thank two of my other colleagues who display that enviable combination of wit and powerful intellect, John Vesey, ACSW, of Grand Rapids, Michigan, public school system; and the renowned psychologist, writer, and trainer, Dr. Jim Sutton, of Pleasanton, Texas.

I am also most pleased to be able to thank my agent, Gareth Esersky, of the Carol Mann Agency (New York, NY), for her guidance in preparing the original proposal for this project, and for shepherding it through to acceptance by Da Capo Press. Her work came during some dark days for the publishing industry. I am aware of how increasingly difficult it is to place a manuscript, and am indebted to her for her efforts.

Likewise, I am pleased to be able to thank Katie McHugh, Executive Editor at Perseus Books Group, for taking on such an unusual project. Her comments during the editing stage, along with those of Erica Truxler, Editorial Assistant, and Cisca Schreefel, Associate Director of Editorial Services, have sharpened the manuscript while at the same time preserving its original voice and intent. I am fortunate to have been able to work with this team.

And finally, I must thank the children and their parents. It is at once both humbling and remarkably flattering to be invited to participate in a child's life. At this late stage in my career, it is clear to me that everything I know about psychology that is worth knowing, I have learned from children.

ABOUT THE AUTHOR

DOUGLAS RILEY is a North Carolina native. He was raised on a farm by loving, tolerant, humorous parents, and there is no doubt that the wit and humor that suffuses his work traces its roots to his early upbringing. He is married and has two sons, Collin and Sam, who are chips off the same humorous block. After all, they had to endure his experiments and tricks throughout their childhood. Bless them!

Dr. Riley is in private practice in Newport News, Virginia, where he specializes in child psychology. He is available for workshops and public presentations, and can be reached at www.drdouglasriley.com.